MOCA-PBR Study Guide &

Test Companion

By Pediatrics Board Review (PBR)

Your <u>Certification</u> <u>SYSTEM</u> for

Passing the Pediatric Boards

- •*100% Money Back Pass Guarantee*•
- •*MASSIVE Online Community*•
- •*Board-Focused, Manageable Content*•
- •*Powerful Mnemonics*•

EFFICIENT LEARNING So You Can

Enjoy Life & Have More Fun!

Written by Ashish Goyal, MD

www.PediatricsBoardReview.com

COPYRIGHT INFORMATION

ISBN 978-1-387-35042-1

HOW SHOULD I USE THE MOCA-PBR ON EXAM DAY?

I strongly recommend that you use the ONLINE version on exam day. My online version of the MOCA-PBR Study Guide & Test Companion has been specially designed to give you the most efficient means to locating your answers to the MOCA-Peds questions. A video shows you exactly how to use the:

- Rephrased topics (Learning Objectives and Featured Readings)
- Alphabetized topics
- On-page search function
- Full study guide search function
- "Jump" links to quickly visit key topic summary sections
- And more...

SHOULD YOU SUBMIT ERRORS TO PBR? YES & NO!

CRITICAL NOTE: Due to the potential appearance of impropriety (i.e., the possibility of changing content throughout the year based on insider knowledge from exam takers), we avoid making any modifications to the study guide based on exam feedback and questions from members.

PLEASE SUBMIT TRUE ERRORS!

True errors include:

1. Factually incorrect information.
2. Conceptually incorrect information (e.g., the Learning Objective said "recognition," but we only discussed the treatment).
3. Major content gaps (e.g., the Learning Objective was about identification of headaches, but completely omitted the subtopic of migraines).

If you find such an error, please help us out by submitting the error through the link below. We will update our online study guide(s) AND we will add the error to our ERRATA page. We may even update our hardcopy books.

www.pbrlinks.com/moca-error

WHAT ABOUT QUESTIONS ABOUT TOPICS, FEEDBACK, & SMALL CONTENT GAPS?

Again, if a true error or omission is noted, definitely submit it to us so that we can quickly address it!

However, if you note a small content gap, or if you have individual, content-specific questions, or suggestions, it's unlikely that we'll feel comfortable assisting with those once the MOCA-PBR Study Guide & Test Companion has officially been published and released.

ERRATA/CORRECTIONS PAGE LOCATION

A running list of content updates and errors will be easily accessible from the www.pbrlinks.com/moca-error error submission page. For any updates and errors that are felt important enough to place on the ERRATA page, we will update our online editions with those changes in a timely manner.

SPECIAL THANKS TO THESE CONTRIBUTORS

A special thanks to these pediatricians for helping to curate content for me:

Jennifer Thompson
John Cole
Janna Flint
Samantha Ball
Katie Stephenson
Marvin Wang

PBR IMAGE LINKS

The image links in the PBR lead to phenomenal images throughout the World Wide Web! BUT these images are located on NON-PBR websites. Some websites go out of business. When this happens, we simply need to replace the image. Typically, no more than 1% of the links within PBR are "bad." We have an excellent system that allows us to change the link on our end, but we need your help when a link "dies." Simply submit any "bad link" through the portal below and we'll take care of it!

www.pediatricsboardreview.com/**BADLINK**

PRODUCT REGISTRATION

As mentioned on the PBR site, we offer a quarterly pass guarantee for the MOCA-PBR. "Money Back" requests may be made within 30 days of the score release date. You must register your product within 90 days after making your initial purchase. For complete details, please visit:
www.pediatricsboardreview.com/guarantee

Visit the following link to register your product(s):
www.pediatricsboardreview.com/register

If you made an official purchase that was initiated through the PBR website, but resulted in your purchase being processed through Lulu.com, Amazon.com, or another authorized distributor of PBR resources, please contact us and submit a copy of your receipt:
www.pediatricsboardreview.com/contact

CME OPPORTUNITIES

DID YOU KNOW THAT YOU MAY QUALIFY FOR A $2000 CASH REBATE?

PLUS...

200 CME CREDITS
200 MOC PART 2 POINTS

VISIT THE FOLLOWING LINK & LEARN MORE NOW!
www.pbrlinks.com/MOCA-CME

2023 MOCA-PEDS GENERAL PEDIATRICS LEARNING OBJECTIVES

For efficiency's sake, we've reworded, and reordered, the Learning Objectives to make the topics easy to find when you're using the MOCA-PBR Study Guide & Test Companion as a test companion.

1. Acne in Adolescents – Managing
2. Adolescent Intimate Partner Violence Understanding Risk Factors, Screening, and Prevention Strategies
3. Allergy Testing (including Skin and In Vitro Tests) – Knowing the Indications and Limitations
4. Asthma - Acute Asthma Exacerbation in Children – Managing
5. Asthma Controller Therapy - Planning
6. Blunt Abdominal Trauma Understanding the Initial Evaluation and Potential Complications
7. Central Nervous System Tumors in Children Understanding the Clinical Manifestations and Differential Diagnosis
8. Chest Pain in Children and Adolescents Understanding the Differential Diagnosis and Evaluation
9. Childhood-Onset Fluency Disorder – Providing Counseling
10. Children Behind on Vaccines or Having an Unknown Vaccination Record – Managing
11. Chronic Illness in the Adolescent/Young Adult – Planning the Transition to Adult Care Provider
12. Common Neonatal Birth Injuries – Recognizing and Managing
13. Common Pediatric Illnesses – Understanding and Applying Return-to-School Criteria
14. Common Viral Exanthems – Recognizing
15. Conjunctivitis in Patients – Evaluating and Managing
16. Dysphagia – Diagnosing and Evaluating
17. Emergency Contraception in Adolescent Patients – Understanding Usage
18. Febrile Seizures – Understanding the Clinical Features, Management, and Prognosis
19. Fetal Alcohol Spectrum Disorder – Understanding the Clinical Features, Approach to Evaluation, and Differential Diagnosis
20. Generalizability of a Research Study – Understanding Influential Factors
21. HIV Exposure in Infants – Evaluating and Managing
22. Hoarseness in Children – Understanding the Common Causes and Management
23. Hypoglycemia in Children – Evaluating and Managing
24. Hypospadias in a Neonate – Recognizing and Managing
25. Introducing Solid Foods (Including Highly Allergenic Foods) to Infants – Understanding Current Recommendations
26. Microcephaly in Infants – Evaluating
27. Microscopic Hematuria in Children – Evaluating
28. Myocarditis – Recognizing the Clinical Manifestations, Etiology, and Diagnosis
29. Oral Health Risks – Screening and Managing Appropriately
30. Parental Refusal of Immunizations or Other Treatments – Recognizing and Applying Ethical Principles
31. Performance-Enhancing Drugs Usage in Adolescent Athletes – Identifying
32. Polydactyly in Infants – Evaluating and Managing
33. Prenatally Diagnosed Hydronephrosis in Infants – Evaluating and Managing
34. Primary Immunodeficiency Disorders – Recognizing the Presentation
35. Rheumatic Fever – Recognizing the Clinical Features

36. Safety and Injury Prevention for School-Age Children (Ages 5-10 Years) – Providing Anticipatory Guidance
37. SARS-CoV-2 Infection in Children – Recognizing the Clinical Manifestations (including Post-Acute Sequelae) and Planning Appropriate Initial Evaluation or Management
38. Self-Injurious Behavior in Adolescents – Managing
39. Sexually Transmitted Infection Testing in Prepubertal and Peripubertal Children – Recognizing Indications
40. Short Stature in Children – Evaluating
41. Sickle Cell Disease Complications: Understanding the Prevention and Management
42. Staring Spells in Children – Planning the Evaluation
43. Status Epilepticus – Recognizing and Planning Initial Management
44. Thrombophilic Disorders – Recognizing the Complications and Implications
45. Vaping or E-cigarette Use – Understanding the Health Risks

2023 MOCA-PEDS GENERAL PEDIATRICS FEATURED READINGS
1. Anxiety Disorders in Children and Adolescents - Assessment and Treatment
2. Asthma Management NIH Guidelines – 2020 Focused Updates
3. Sudden Death in the Young
4. Well-Appearing Febrile Infants 8 to 60 Days Old - Evaluation and Management

The original phrasing of the Learning Objectives and Featured Readings from the ABP are available here: https://www.abp.org/mocapeds

TABLE OF CONTENTS

Topic 1: Acne in Adolescents – Managing
Manage acne in an adolescent patient

BACKGROUND

Acne vulgaris affects 85% of adolescents and may persist well into a patient's 30s. It is a disease of the pilosebaceous unit, which is a tetrad of inflammation, shedding of keratinocytes, increased sebum, and Cutibacterium (formerly known as Proprionibacterium acnes). Acne can lead to long-lasting post inflammatory hyperpigmentation, embarrassment, and permanent scarring if not treated appropriately.

CLASSIFICATION

COMEDONAL

Results in skin-colored papules frequently seen on the forehead and chin.
IMAGE: www.pbrlinks.com/2023MOCA-COMEDONAL

INFLAMMATORY

Results in red-colored papules, pustules, nodules, or pseudocysts that are painful and often found on the face as well as the back and chest.
IMAGE: www.pbrlinks.com/2023MOCA-INFLAMMATORY

MIXED COMEDONAL/INFLAMMATORY

As the name suggests, this is a mix of comedonal and inflammatory acne.
IMAGE: www.pbrlinks.com/2023MOCA-MIXED

MANAGEMENT

GENERAL MANAGEMENT

- Use an over the counter (OTC) oil-free face wash every night before bed
- Use OTC benzoyl peroxide +/- OTC topical retinoid
- Encourage sun protection
- Avoid comedogenic cosmetics and moisturizers
- Avoid picking at lesions due to risk for scarring

MANAGEMENT BASED ON ACNE SEVERITY

Acne treatments are focused on targeting one or more components of the pathophysiologic tetrad and can be managed based on **acne severity** or **acne morphology**.
IMAGE: www.pbrlinks.com/2023MOCA-ACNE-GRADES

MILD ACNE

Limited disease with non-inflammatory comedones +/- minimal inflammatory lesions. Treat with topical benzoyl peroxide (BPO), topical antibiotics, +/- topical retinoids.

MODERATE ACNE

Increased spread (chest/back) with more inflammatory lesions. Treat with topical +/- systemic treatment (oral antibiotic and/or oral contraceptive pill - OCP).

SEVERE ACNE

Mostly inflammatory lesions with high risk of scarring and nodulocystic disease. Treat with oral isotretinoin.

MANAGEMENT BASED ON ACNE MORPHOLOGY

MOSTLY COMEDONAL
Treat with topical retinoid +/- benzoyl peroxide (BPO).
IMAGE: www.pbrlinks.com/2023MOCA-COMEDONAL

MOSTLY INFLAMMATORY
Treat with topical antibiotics +/- benzoyl peroxide (BPO).
IMAGE: www.pbrlinks.com/2023MOCA-INFLAMMATORY

MIXED COMEDONAL/INFLAMMATORY
Treat with:
- Oral medications (oral antibiotic +/- oral contraceptives) or,
- Topical retinoid + topical benzoyl peroxide +/- topical or oral antibiotic +/- oral contraceptives

IMAGE: www.pbrlinks.com/MIXED

ACNE MEDICATION MANAGEMENT

ANTI-INFLAMMATORY MEDICATION
- Benzoyl peroxide (BPO) 2.5% to 10% (gels work best and 5% is sufficient for most)

TOPICAL ANTIBIOTICS
- Clindamycin or erythromycin are usually combined with BPO or retinoid product.
- Dapsone 5%-7.5% gel (inhibits bacterial synthesis of folic acid and is anti-inflammatory)

TOPICAL RETINOIDS
- Tretinoin (1st generation). This is used at nighttime only due to extreme photosensitivity.
- Tazarotene and Adapalene (3rd generation). These have less light sensitivity and are often combined with BPO.
- Educate the patient that the first month of treatment can lead to paradoxical worsening of acne due to loosening of deeper comedones that come to the surface.

SYSTEMIC ANTIBIOTICS
- Never use as monotherapy and limit use to avoid antibiotic resistance
- Doxycycline QD – BID, or use the extended-release version
- Minocycline QD for 12 weeks
    - Major adverse effects to minocycline lead many clinicians to avoid this medication. Such adverse effects include minocycline-induced lupus like reaction, pseudotumor cerebri (when used in combination with isotretinoin), drug reaction with eosinophilia and systemic symptoms (DRESS).

HORMONE MEDICATIONS
- Oral contraceptive pills (OCP) in postmenarchal females, including:
    - Androgen synthesis inhibitors: Estrogen and progesterone combination OCP
    - Androgen receptor antagonists: Spironolactone, flutamide, and cyproterone acetate

"OTHER" MEDICATION
- Isotretinoin (exact mechanism unknown)
    - Oral retinoid that affects all components of the acne tetrad with curative potential

- o Given over 20 weeks
- o Monitor labs (cholesterol and liver function) monthly for 3 months, then every 3 months until treatment is complete due to potential for increased levels of triglycerides, increased cholesterol, and hepatotoxicity.
- o Screen all females for pregnancy monthly due to **teratogenic effects** on the fetus

MANAGEMENT CONSIDERATIONS IN SPECIAL POPULATIONS

PREADOLESCENT CHILDREN (< 12 YEARS OLD)
- Avoid oral tetracyclines in children up to age 8 years old.
- Avoid oral contraceptive pills (OCPs) until one year after the onset of menstruation due to the possibility of diminished growth and bone density.

PREGNANT INDIVIDUALS
- Contraindications include isotretinoin and topical tazarotene (retinoid) due to teratogenic effects on the fetus
- Avoid oral tetracyclines and topical minocycline due to the potential for tooth discoloration in the fetus.
- Insufficient evidence to support the safety of topical clascoterone (hormonal anti-androgen medication) and topical dapsone (antibiotic/anti-inflammatory medication)

HIGHLY PIGMENTED SKIN COLORED INDIVIDUALS
Darker skinned patients are more likely to develop treatment-induced postinflammatory hyperpigmentation (PIH). To limit the possibility of this:
- Start with lower concentrations of retinoid and slowly titrate up the frequency of use.
- Consider the use a benzoyl peroxide wash rather than a gel to minimize the amount of time the medication is in contact with the skin.

HYPERANDROGENISM ASSOCIATED DISEASES
Diseases such as polycystic ovarian syndrome, late-onset adrenal hyperplasia, adrenal tumors, or ovarian tumors can contribute to acne.

ACNE EXCORIEE
This is also known as "picker's acne," in which individuals have a compulsion to pick, squeeze, and scratch acne lesions and scabs. This requires psychological treatment.

REFERENCES
https://publications.aap.org/pediatricsinreview/article/40/11/577/35248/Acne-Vulgaris-in-the-Pediatric-Patient
https://publications.aap.org/pediatricsinreview/article/34/11/479/34762/Acne-and-Its-Management
https://www.uptodate.com/contents/acne-vulgaris-overview-of-management

Topic 2: Adolescent Intimate Partner Violence - Understanding Risk Factors, Screening, and Prevention Strategies

Understand risk factors, screening, and prevention strategies for adolescent intimate partner violence

BACKGROUND

Adolescent intimate partner violence is a major public health concern because it can lead to consequences such as **unintentional pregnancies, STDs, physical injuries, mental health issues,** and **academic problems**. It is important to consider the risk factors and screen patients in order to provide strategies to help prevent these issues from occurring.

RISK FACTORS AND PROTECTIVE FACTORS

RISK FACTORS

Risk factors for becoming a victim of adolescent intimate partner violence include **childhood abuse** (physical or sexual), early puberty, early coitarche (first sexual intercourse at 13 years of age or younger), **substance use**, pregnancy, being postpartum, sexting, **sexual minority orientation**, low socioeconomic status, being under child protective services or foster care, being involved in the juvenile justice system, and **homelessness**.

PROTECTIVE FACTORS

Protective factors against becoming a victim of adolescent intimate partner violence include family and school **support**, involvement in **social or community activities**, positive parenting exposure, **communication skills, knowledge of consent**, and participating in **prevention programs**.

WARNING SIGNS

Physicians should look out for **warning signs** that their patient may be a victim of intimate partner violence. These include signs of **trauma, physical injury**, vague and **nonspecific complaints** (fatigue, sleep issues, headaches, abdominal pain), **mental health issues** (anxiety, depression, suicidal ideation), **substance abuse**, frequent requests for **pregnancy tests or STD screening**, frequent use of **emergency contraceptives**, multiple **abortions**, being sexually active with **older or multiple partners, early first intercourse at ≤ 13 years of age**, and a **partner who refuses to leave the patient's room** during a healthcare visit.

SCREENING

Physicians should do **psychosocial screens for adolescents at every routine healthcare visit.** The most common is the **"HEADSS" assessment**, which asks patients about **their home, education, activities, drug use, sexual activity**, and any **suicidal ideations**. When discussing sexual activity, physicians can ask if the patient feels safe in their relationship and whether they have ever been abused. The **"FISTS" assessment** can also be used to screen for violence by asking the adolescent directly about their involvement in **fights, injuries, sexual violence, threats, and self-defense**.

PREVENTION STRATEGIES

UNIVERSAL EDUCATION AND ANTICIPITORY GUIDANCE

Physicians should **educate all patients** about **healthy relationships** and **provide counseling** about intimate partner violence **regardless of whether the patient has risk factors or not**. By openly discussing the topic at each healthcare visit, physicians can **reduce the stigma** and help patients feel more comfortable about disclosing information regarding their relationships and let patients know that they have their **support**.

UNIVERSAL INQUIRY

Physicians should **ask about intimate partner violence** during the visit in a non-judgmental way that would not make the patient feel shameful. One example would be to **bring awareness** to the patient about the topic by letting the patient know that some people may experience intimate partner violence and then proceed to ask if they have ever experienced something like that before themselves. The more often this question is asked, the more it becomes normalized and the more likely the patient will be to come ask for help if the need arises. For patients with risk factors, asking further questions that are **both open-ended and specific** is recommended.

UNIVERSAL PROVISION OF RESOURCES

Since some patients may not feel comfortable discussing intimate partner violence with their physician, **all patients should be made aware of the resources that are available to them**. Some examples include **domestic violence and rape crisis centers, child protection services**, and **mental health counselors and therapists**. These resources can be **local or national**, such as the National Domestic Violence Hotline. Including information about these resources on posters or cards **in patient bathrooms** has started to become common practice since some patients may not feel comfortable discussing these topics just yet.

REFERENCES

https://www.uptodate.com/contents/adolescent-relationship-abuse-including-physical-and-sexual-teen-dating-violence
https://www.uptodate.com/contents/peer-violence-and-violence-prevention
https://publications.aap.org/pediatricsinreview/article-abstract/41/2/73/35370

Topic 3: Allergy Testing (including Skin and In Vitro Tests) – Knowing the Indications and Limitations

Know the indications and limitations of allergy testing (including skin and in vitro tests)

BACKGROUND

Allergy testing should only be initiated after careful history and physical exam. Allergy testing can aid in the diagnosis, but it is not diagnostic. IgE mediated reactions develop within minutes to 2 hours after exposure to a suspected allergen.

Diagnosing an allergy to a specific allergen requires IgE reaction though skin or in vitro testing **and verification that exposure results in symptoms**.

Skin testing and in vitro testing have their limitations and a positive skin test is generally **not specific** enough to make the diagnosis.

SKIN TESTING

INDICATIONS FOR SKIN TESTING

Skin testing is excellent for aeroallergens (airborne allergens), but may also be used for other allergens.

- Allergic asthma, rhinitis, and conjunctivitis
- Allergies to trees, grasses, wheat, molds, and animal proteins (pet dander and insects like cockroaches)
- Some medication allergies (only validated for penicillin)
- Venom allergies (i.e., wasps, hornets, yellow jackets, fire ants, and others)

ADVANTAGES

- Rapid and cost effective. Generally, results are made within 15-30 minutes
- Considered fairly reliable for airborne substances (e.g., pollen, pet dander, and dust mites)
- Easy to perform
- The negative predictive value for foods and inhalants is excellent

DISADVANTAGES/LIMITATIONS

- False negatives can occur when patients are on an antihistamine or antidepressant
- The positive predictive value is not good for foods (i.e., may produces many false positive results). Therefore, skin testing for food allergies may often result in addition tests being needed (e.g., a oral food challenge).
- Not recommended for those at high risk for anaphylactic reactions or skin conditions such as dermographism and atopic dermatitis
- Can be very itchy and uncomfortable

IN-VITRO TESTING

INDICATIONS

Radioallergosorbent testing (RAST testing) is blood testing. RAST testing may be used for aeroallergens, such as pollen, mold, dander, cockroach, and it is more appropriate for:

- Food allergies
- Allergies to insect venoms

- Confirming negative skin tests results when there is a high index of suspicion for a particular allergy
- Confirming a positive skin test for food and venom allergies

ADVANTAGES
- Not affected by taking antihistamines or antidepressants
- No risk to those who are high risk of allergic reaction or anaphylaxis
- Less uncomfortable
- Can be used for latex allergy
- Not affected by skin diseases or skin integrity. Can be performed in as young as 6 weeks of age.

DISADVANTAGES/LIMITATIONS
- Less sensitive and more costly than skin testing
- Test results are delayed
- Fewer allergens are tested

REFERENCES
https://www.uptodate.com/contents/overview-of-in-vitro-allergy-tests
https://www.uptodate.com/contents/overview-of-skin-testing-for-IgE-mediated-allergic-disease
https://www.contemporarypediatrics.com/view/allergy-testing-children-which-test-when

Topic 4: Asthma - Acute Asthma Exacerbation in Children – Managing
Manage a child with an acute asthma exacerbation

BACKGROUND
Asthma is a chronic inflammatory condition of the airways characterized by 3 features, including airflow obstruction, bronchial hyperresponsiveness, and underlying inflammation. During an asthma exacerbation, the airways narrow and slow the speed of air moving into the lungs. **A peak flow meter (PFM) can help show narrowing of the airways well before an asthma exacerbation happens**. A peak flow measurement should be done 1 or more times daily (at the same time of day), or whenever there are early signs of an asthma exacerbation.

DEFINING THE SEVERITY OF AN ACUTE ASTHMA EXACERBATION
The following are the "zones" and the related symptoms that can help care providers and family members recognize if the child is doing well or is having an asthma exacerbation:

- **GREEN ZONE ("GO")**: No acute exacerbation. Patient is doing well with no symptoms of coughing, wheezing, chest tightness, or shortness of breath. Can do usual activities. **Peak flow is 80%-100% of the highest reading**.
- **YELLOW ZONE ("CAUTION")**: Some symptoms of cough, wheezing, chest tightness, breathing difficulties, or waking up at night due to coughing. Some limitations to usual activities. **Peak flow is 50%-80% of the highest reading**.
- **RED ZONE ("STOP")**: Severe symptoms including shortness of breath, **quick-relief medicines do not help**, or symptoms are the same or worse after 24 hours in the yellow zone. **Peak flow is < 50% of the highest reading. THIS IS AN EMERGENCY.**

ASTHMA MEDICATIONS
Quick-relief medications (albuterol and levalbuterol) are the short-acting beta agonists (SABAs), which are bronchodilators that work within minutes and may be effective for 4-6 hours. They are used at home, school, clinic, or in the ED for asthma exacerbations. They are **not** for daily use and are typically used when a child is in the yellow or red zone. Albuterol tends to cause more tachycardia than levalbuterol. Ipratropium is a short-acting muscarinic antagonist (SAMA) and is typically used in combination with a SABA during an acute asthma exacerbation.

Long-term controller medications are used daily for maintenance of asthma control. These medications do not provide immediate relief.

- **Inhaled corticosteroids** (fluticasone, budesonide, mometasone, beclomethasone, ciclesonide) are anti-inflammatory medications that reduce the swelling and tightening of airways. They may need to be used for weeks to months before getting maximum benefit.
- **Leukotriene modifiers** (montelukast, zafirlukast, zileuton) block the effects of leukotrienes, which are immune system molecules that cause asthma symptoms. These medications can help prevent symptoms for up to 24 hours.
- **Long-acting beta agonists (aka LABAs)** (salmeterol and formoterol) are bronchodilators and reduce swelling for at least 12 hours and are used to control moderate to severe asthma and prevent nighttime symptoms. The onset of action is significantly longer than that of SABAs.
- **Long-acting muscarinic antagonists aka LAMAs** (tiotropium) are bronchodilators and used to control severe asthma when an LABA cannot be used.

Severe asthma exacerbation medications (Red Zone)

- **Ipratropium** and is often used in combination with a SABA (**albuterol or levalbuterol**).
- **Oral glucocorticoids** (prednisone or methylprednisolone) are steroid medications used to treat severe asthma exacerbations.
  - <u>**PEARL**</u>: A home dose of emergency oral corticosteroids can lead to decreased ED use in children with moderate to severe asthma with close physician consultation.
- **Terbutaline** is a beta agonist that is a fast-acting bronchodilator.
- **Magnesium sulfate** relaxes smooth muscles in the bronchioles.
- **Inhaled epinephrine** is an alpha- and beta-adrenergic agonist that relaxes airway muscles to control bronchospasm.

MANAGEMENT AT HOME/SCHOOL BASED ON ASTHMA ACTION PLANS

GREEN ZONE → Doing well

- Continue taking long-term control medicine

YELLOW ZONE → Asthma is getting worse with peak flow meter at ½ to ¾ of best peak flow reading

- Repeated administration of short-acting beta-agonists (SABAs)
  - 2-4 puffs with a spacer every 4 hours
- Continue long-term control medicine

RED ZONE → Medical alert! Peak flow meter is < ½ of best peak flow reading

- Repeated administration of short-acting beta-agonists (SABAs)
  - 4-8 puffs with a spacer every 15 minutes x 3 while on the way to the ED
- High-dose inhaled-corticosteroids (ICS) are **NOT** effective for red zone management

MANAGEMENT IN THE EMERGENCY ROOM

MILD EXACERBATION

Symptoms may include normal alertness, tachypnea, expiratory wheezing, accessory muscle use, and O2 saturations > 95%.

- Give **SABAs** such as albuterol via nebulizer or metered dose inhaler (MDI) x 3 doses every 20 minutes.
- Give **oral glucocorticoids** (prednisolone/prednisone or dexamethasone) if there is no improvement after one inhalation therapy or if there is a history of severe or recurrent exacerbations.
- Note that transient hypoxia due to ventilation-perfusion mismatch is common after bronchodilator use.

MODERATE EXACERBATION

Symptoms may include normal alertness, tachypnea, wheezing (expiratory +/- inspiratory), accessory muscle use, and O2 saturations in the 92-95% range.

- Give **nebulized albuterol + ipratropium** x 3 doses every 20 minutes or continuously for one hour
- Give **oral glucocorticoids** within 30-60 minutes of ED arrival

SEVERE EXACERBATION

Symptoms include inability to repeat a short phrase, extreme tachypnea, wheezing (expiratory **and** inspiratory), heavy use of accessory muscles, and O2 saturations < 92% on room air.

- Give continuous **nebulized albuterol + ipratropium** for the 1st hour and then consider transition to continuous nebulized albuterol.
- Give **IV methylprednisolone** as soon as IV access is established.
- Consider **IM/IV terbutaline or epinephrine** for very poor inspiratory flow.
- Consider giving **IV magnesium sulfate** as this has been shown to reduce the risk of hospitalization.

MANAGING IMPENDING RESPIRATORY FAILURE

Symptoms of impending respiratory failure include an inability to maintain respiratory effort, cyanosis, inability to speak, altered mental status, PaCO2 $\geq$ 42 mm Hg, respiratory acidosis, and O2 sat < 90%. Do not delay intubation once deemed necessary.

- Give **IV terbutaline** and continuous **nebulized albuterol**.
- Start **IV methylprednisolone** as soon as IV access is established.
- Consider giving **IM/IV epinephrine**.
- Consider giving **IV magnesium sulfate**.
- **Ventilatory support** (poor ventilation causes acidosis from hypercarbia)
  - Noninvasive positive pressure ventilation (NPPV)
  - Intubation (use with caution in status asthmaticus as airway manipulation can lead to increased airflow obstruction due to exaggerated bronchial responsiveness)

REFERENCES

https://publications.aap.org/pediatricsinreview/article/40/11/549/35239
https://www.uptodate.com/contents/acute-asthma-exacerbations-in-children-younger-than-12-years-emergency-department-management
https://www.nhlbi.nih.gov/science/national-asthma-education-and-prevention-program-naepp
https://www.cdc.gov/asthma/action-plan/documents/asthma-action-plan-508.pdf

Topic 5: Asthma Controller Therapy - Planning

Plan the appropriate use of controller therapy in a patient with asthma.

BACKGROUND

Controller therapy is used on a daily basis to prevent asthma symptoms over the long term. For this MOCA-Peds Learning Objective, **you could be asked to plan the initial therapy, to step up therapy, or step down therapy** based on a child's symptoms. Please note that a child's **asthma severity classification** (e.g., mild persistent) is based on the severity of the disease when the patient initially presents and is not on any asthma medications. The concept of **asthma control** has to do with how well a patient's asthma is controlled while under therapy.

The **initial therapy** for a child is determined by the asthma severity classification. Therapy may include daily controller medications. **Modifications of controller medications** are then made in a stepwise fashion based on how well the asthma is controlled.

Knowing the following abbreviations will be very helpful: ICS, inhaled corticosteroid; OCS, oral corticosteroid; LABA, long-acting beta2-agonist; SABA, inhaled short-acting beta2-agonist; RTI, respiratory tract infection; PRN, as needed; LTRA, leukotriene receptor antagonist; LAMA, long-acting muscarinic antagonist

APPROACH TO ASTHMA CONTROLLER THERAPY QUESTIONS

Please consider the following approach to MOCA-Peds questions about controller therapy:

- **Check the patient's age** and visit the corresponding section in this topic summary.
- **If asked to initiate therapy**, click the related **INITIATE** URL provided.
- **If asked to manage existing therapy:**
  - Assess asthma control with the related **CONTROL** URL provided.
  - Prior to stepping up, **ALWAYS check the patient's** compliance with scheduled medications, inhaler technique, environmental control, and comorbid conditions. Also, if the patient is on an alternative treatment regimen, **switch to the preferred treatment regimen** for the corresponding step.
  - If based on the level of control it seems therapy may need to be stepped up or down, click the related **STEP** URL provided to see what the appropriate next step up or down should be.

0 TO 4 YEAR OLDS – INITIATING OR MANAGING CONTROLLER MEDICATIONS

- For help **initiating therapy** based on asthma severity levels, click the following link:
  - www.pbrlinks.com/2023MOCA-INITIATE1 **(Use the left, NAEPP side of the table)**
- **Assess asthma control** and decide if therapy should be maintained, stepped up, or stepped down by clicking the following link:
  - www.pbrlinks.com/2023MOCA-CONTROL1 **(Review the "Recommended action for treatment" row)**
- To **see the steps** for this age group, click the following link:
  - www.pbrlinks.com/2023MOCA-STEP1

Prior to stepping up therapy, ALWAYS check the patient's compliance with scheduled medications, inhaler technique, environmental control, and comorbid conditions. Also, if the patient is on an alternative treatment regimen, **switch to the preferred treatment regimen** for the corresponding step. After stepping up, **reassess in 4-6 weeks.**

Prior to stepping down, make sure the patient has had at least **3 consecutive months** of well-controlled asthma.

Consider a consultation with a specialist if the patient is at Step 2. **Obtain a consultation at Step 3.**

5 TO 11 YEAR OLDS – INITIATING OR MANAGING CONTROLLER MEDICATIONS

- For help **initiating therapy** based on asthma severity levels, click the following link:
  - www.pbrlinks.com/2023MOCA-INITIATE2 (**Use the left, NAEPP side of the table**)
- **Assess asthma control** and decide if therapy should be maintained, stepped up, or stepped down by clicking the following link:
  - www.pbrlinks.com/2023MOCA-CONTROL2 (**Review the "Recommended action for treatment" row**)
- To **see the steps** for this age group, click the following link:
  - www.pbrlinks.com/2023MOCA-STEP2

Prior to stepping up therapy, ALWAYS check the patient's compliance with scheduled medications, inhaler technique, environmental control, and comorbid conditions. Also, if the patient is on an alternative treatment regimen, **switch to the preferred treatment regimen** for the corresponding step. After stepping up, **reassess in 2-6 weeks.**

Prior to stepping down, make sure the patient has had at least **3 consecutive months** of well-controlled asthma.

Consider a consultation with a specialist if the patient is at Step 3. **Obtain a consultation at Step 4.**

12 YEAR OLDS & OLDER CHILDREN – INITIATING OR MANAGING CONTROLLER MEDICATIONS

- For help **initiating therapy** based on asthma severity levels, click the following link:
  - www.pbrlinks.com/2023MOCA-INITIATE3 (**Use the left, NAEPP side of the table**)
- **Assess asthma control** and decide if therapy should be maintained, stepped up, or stepped down by clicking the following link and **increasing by 1 step if** asthma is "not well controlled" and **by 2 steps if** asthma is "poorly controlled":
  - www.pbrlinks.com/2023MOCA-CONTROL3
- To **see the steps** for this age group, click the following link:
  - www.pbrlinks.com/2023MOCA-STEP3

Prior to stepping up therapy, ALWAYS check the patient's compliance with scheduled medications, inhaler technique, environmental control, and comorbid conditions. Also, if the patient is on an alternative treatment regimen, **switch to the preferred treatment regimen** for the corresponding step. After stepping up, **reassess in 2-6 weeks.**

Prior to stepping down, make sure the patient has had at least **3 consecutive months** of well-controlled asthma.

Consider a consultation with a specialist if the patient is at Step 3. **Obtain a consultation at Step 4**

REFERENCES

https://www.uptodate.com/contents/asthma-in-children-younger-than-12-years-management-of-persistent-asthma-with-controller-therapies

https://www.uptodate.com/contents/asthma-in-children-younger-than-12-years-overview-of-initiating-therapy-and-monitoring-control

https://www.uptodate.com/contents/treatment-of-intermittent-and-mild-persistent-asthma-in-adolescents-and-adults

https://www.uptodate.com/contents/an-overview-of-asthma-management

https://www.uptodate.com/contents/asthma-in-children-younger-than-12-years-initial-evaluation-and-diagnosis

2020 Focused Updates to the Asthma Management Guidelines: A Report from the National Asthma Education and Prevention Program Coordinating Committee Expert Panel Working Group

Topic 6: Blunt Abdominal Trauma - Understanding the Initial Evaluation and Potential Complications

Understand the initial evaluation and potential complications of blunt abdominal trauma

BACKGROUND

Children are at increased risk of intra-abdominal injury (IAI). This is due to their:
- Relatively larger surface area of the abdomen (larger impactable target)
- Relatively smaller abdominal wall muscle mass/fat (less protection)
- Relatively larger solid organ size (especially liver and spleen)

Most Common Injuries (in order):
- Solid Organs: liver, spleen, kidneys
- Hollow Viscous Organs: intestines
- Abdominal Vasculature

While **death from IAI is rare**, the greater the number of structures that are injured, the higher the mortality risk. If the vasculature is injured, the mortality risk increases to 50%.

INITIAL EVALUATION

Start by determining whether the patient is hemodynamically stable or unstable. If UNSTABLE, then proceed to emergency laparotomy. **If STABLE**, continue the evaluation with a history, physical exam, possible laboratory studies, and possible radiological studies.

HEMODYNAMICALLY UNSTABLE

Look for **signs of hemodynamic instability**, including abnormal blood pressure, abnormal heart rate, cold extremities, prolonged capillary refill, altered mental status (or loss of consciousness), and shortness of breath.

If the patient is unstable, radiological tests **should not be done if they will delay surgery**. However, if time allows, consider an **eFAST (Extended Focused Assessment with Sonography in Trauma) exam**. This gives a rapid view of all four quadrants, looking for hemopericardium and/or intraperitoneal fluid. If quickly available, it can be done by the bedside preoperatively. **CT scan of the abdomen and pelvis** may also be considered.

HEMODYNAMICALLY STABLE

Obtain a history of the trauma including the mechanism of injury. Factors to consider:
- Was it a high energy blow (e.g., fall onto a bike handlebar)?
  - **IMAGE**: www.pbrlinks.com/2023MOCA-HANDLEBAR
- Was it related to a motor vehicle accident (with or without seatbelt)?
- Was the fall from > 10 feet or 2-3 times the patient's height?
- Are there any reports of abdominal pain?

Complete a physical exam and look for evidence of potential IAI, including:
- Ecchymoses (bruising)
- Abrasions
- Tire track marks

- Seat belt sign
  - **IMAGE**: www.pbrlinks.com/2023MOCA-SEATBELT
- Abdominal tenderness
- Abdominal distention
- Peritoneal irritation (e.g., abdominal wall rigidity, rebound, guarding, or Kehr's sign in which there is left shoulder pain while palpating the left upper abdominal quadrant)
- Absent bowel signs (indicates prolonged ileus)
- Lower rib tenderness (could mean there's a rib fracture and possible hepatic/splenic injury)

Laboratory evaluations may include some of the following when there is concern for IAI:
- Complete blood count (CBC): MEASURE FREQUENTLY while monitoring exam (every 4-6hours).
- Blood type and crossmatch
- Serum transaminases (AST/ALT)
- Serum electrolytes, creatinine, blood urea nitrogen (BUN)
- Blood glucose
- Amylase and lipase
- Prothrombin time/Prothrombin time (PT/PTT)
- Urinalysis
- Urine or serum pregnancy testing
- Alcohol/drug testing

Radiological evaluations may include:
- **Ultrasonography (eFAST)**: Discussed above. Please note that it is poorly sensitive and specific for solid organ and hollow viscous injury. Therefore, interpret these results in conjunction with the clinical picture.
- **Contrast-enhanced ultrasound (CEUS)**: This has greater sensitivity (almost as good as CT) in determining solid organ injury. This has not been studied as extensively.
- **CT of the Abdominal and Pelvis**: Obtained in hemodynamically STABLE children with high clinical suspicion for IAI based on exam and/or lab work. Use IV contrast. Consider also obtaining when there is altered sensorium limiting a good physical exam, the eFast is positive, chest x-ray shows a possible hemoperitoneum or pneumoperitoneum, there are other serious injuries which may be associated with IAI (e.g., long bone injury or other torso injury), and if there are abnormal labs (e.g., increased AST/ALT, increased pancreatic enzymes, significant hematuria, declining hematocrit).

MANAGEMENT

HEMODYNAMICALLY UNSTABLE
If the patient is unstable, get a CBC, crossmatch, and take the patient to the OR. As mentioned above, an eFAST (Extended Focused Assessment with Sonography in Trauma) exam and CT scan of the abdomen and pelvis may be considered, but radiological tests should not be done if they will delay surgery.

HEMODYNAMICALLY STABLE
Serial exams are done when there is concern for IAI. Monitor for concerning trends in the patient's signs and symptoms. In a "**secondary survey**" (a repeat exam thoroughly looking for additional significant

injuries), also check the genitalia and perineum to look for possible pelvic, rectal, urethral, and vaginal injuries. A digital rectal exam is not necessary unless there is suspicion of spinal cord injury.

If the patient arrives with a history that is consistent with low risk for intra-abdominal injury, including the LACK of abdominal pain, a seat belt sign, physical trauma, other signs/symptoms mentioned above, and the patient is hemodynamically stable, has normal labs, and has normal serial exams, the patient can likely be discharged.

If the patient's exam has any signs/symptoms that are concerning for IAI, obtain a CT of the abdomen and pelvis. This is the priority over the lab work. If serial exams and all evaluations are negative, then discharge.

COMPLICATIONS

The above content contains some potential complications. Additional complications have been listed here for easy reference.

Hemodynamic instability as evidenced by:
- Abnormal blood pressure
- Abnormal heart rate
- Cold extremities
- Prolonged capillary refill
- Altered mental status
- Shortness of Breath or Respiratory distress

Solid organ trauma may lead to organ loss and hemodynamic instability. Organs to keep in mind include the:
- Liver
- Kidneys
- Spleen
- Pancreas
- Hollow viscous organs (can lead to peritonitis, abscess formation, death)

Abdominal vasculature disruption may lead to:
- Blood loss
- Hemodynamic instability
- Death

REFERENCES
https://www.uptodate.com/contents/pediatric-blunt-abdominal-trauma-initial-evaluation-and-stabilization

Topic 7: Central Nervous System Tumors in Children - Understanding the Clinical Manifestations and Differential Diagnosis

Understand the clinical manifestations and differential diagnosis of central nervous system tumors in children

BACKGROUND

CNS tumors are the most common solid organ tumor in childhood, and the leading cause of childhood death from cancer. The manifestations can vary based on the age of the child and the location of the tumor.

CLINICAL MANIFESTATIONS BY AGE

Headache is the most common symptom, and if present with another concerning symptom, it is suggestive of a brain tumor and should be investigated further.

- **Infants and Young Children < 4 Years**: headache, delayed closure of cranial sutures, bluging fontanelles, macrocephaly, irritability, nausea, emesis, weight loss, poor growth, loss of milestones or developmental delay, seizures, head tilt/torticollis
- **Older Children**: headaches, nausea, emesis, abnormal gait, poor coordination, seizures, papilledema, cranial nerve palsies, hemiplegia, altered consciousness

CLINICAL MANIFESTATIONS BY TUMOR TYPE & LOCATION

The clinical manifestations can vary depending on where a tumor is present. The following is a list of CNS tumor locations and the potential manifestations:

- **Hypothalamus**: endocrine-related diseases such diabetes insipidus or slow growth
- **Optic Pathway**: visual impairment (hemianopsia), proptosis, nystagmus
- **Cerebral Cortex**: headache, seizures, abnormal speech, memory deficits, personality changes, hyperreflexia
- **Posterior Fossa**: nausea and emesis likely, headache, ataxia, abnormal gait or poor coordination, papilledema
- **Brainstem:** abnormal gait, difficulties with coordination, nystagmus, cranial nerve deficits, headache (uncommon), papilledema, torticollis in young children
- **Spinal Cord:** pain and/or weakness corresponding to level of lesion, urinary/bowel incontinence, abnormal gait, torticollis in young children

SPECIFIC SYMPTOMS, PATTERNS, AND ASSOCIATIONS

Certain clusters of symptoms and signs are more suggestive of particular CNS tumor types and CNS tumor locations.

- **Headache**: Most common presenting symptom for a **brain tumor**, but present in only about a 1/3 of children with CNS tumors. The classic pattern includes early morning headaches 42causing a child to waken from sleep or causing a headache upon waking. Headaches are often relived by vomiting. In young children they may not be able to articulate their symptoms, so headaches may present as irritability. The CNS-tumor-associated headaches are thought to be related to rising ICP, so other symptoms such as emesis, vision impairment, growth impairment, lack of coordination or unsteady gait, or changes in school performance may be present as well
- **Nausea/Emesis**: Recurrent or persistent. Possible brain tumor, especially a **posterior fossa tumor** (even with isolated nausea and vomiting).

- **Seizures:** Associated with **supratentorial lesions**.
- **Cranial Nerve Palsies:** These are particularly seen in **brainstem CNS tumors** and may result in a facial palsy, drooling, double vision, or swallowing difficulties. Younger children may cover one eye or tilt their head to alleviate double vision.
- **Torticollis/Head Tilt:** Sudden onset of atraumatic torticollis may be the presenting sign of a CNS tumor, particularly a **posterior fossa or cervical spinal cord tumor**. Interestingly, the torticollis often resolves after surgical treatment.
- **Papilledema:** Optic nerve pallor may be observed on fundus exam due to rising ICP. This may be seen in children with **posterior fossa tumors**.
- **Endocrinopathies:** Midline tumors such as **craniopharyngiomas** are particularly likely to cause diabetes insipidus, growth impairment, precocious puberty, or obesity.
- **Early Hand Preference:** May indicate unilateral weakness or loss of coordination, and may indicate a **CNS tumor in the cortex, brainstem, or spine**.
- **Skin Exam:** Certain cancer predisposition syndromes have accompanying skin findings. For example, **neurofibromatosis type 1** patients typically have axillary freckling and café au lait macules. These patients have an increased risk of **optic pathway gliomas**. Patients with **neurofibromatosis type** 2 are at increased risk of develop **meningiomas and acoustic schwannomas**. Patients with **tuberous sclerosis complex** are at increased risk to develop subependymal **giant cell tumors**.

DIFFERENTIAL DIAGNOSIS

Here are some additional diagnoses that should kept in mind which may have symptoms that overlap with CNS tumors:

- Brain abscesses
- Intracranial hemorrhage
- Hydrocephalus (non-neoplastic)
- Aneurysm
- AV malformations
- Developmental and/or behavioral problems
- Viral gastroenteritis
- Migraine headaches, etc.

REFERENCES

https://www.uptodate.com/contents/clinical-manifestations-and-diagnosis-of-central-nervous-system-tumors-in-children
Katherine C. Pehlivan, Megan R. Paul, John R. Crawford; Central Nervous System Tumors in Children. Pediatr Rev January 2022; 43 (1): 3–15.

Topic 8: Chest Pain in Children and Adolescents - Understanding the Differential Diagnosis and Evaluation

Understand the differential diagnosis and evaluation of chest pain in children and adolescents

BACKGROUND

More than 98% of children and adolescents complain of chest pain at some point. The **vast majority of chest pain in children is of a non-cardiac origin**. The prevalence of cardiac chest pain in children is less than 6%. The differential for cardiac and non-cardiac chest pain is quite wide and is shared below.

GENERAL EVALUATION FOR CHEST PAIN

SYSTEM	SIGNS/SYMPTOMS/HX	PHYSICAL EXAM	LABS/IMAGING
MUSCULOSKELETAL	Reproducible chest pain on the rib cage	Point tenderness (dull or sharp) that can develop gradually or start suddenly	CXR to look for bony lesions
PULMONARY	Increased work of breathing, increased cough, and dyspnea, severe sudden chest pain	Wheezes, crackles, rhonchi, and hypoxia	CXR to look for lung pathology, collapsed lung, or radiodensity
GASTROINTESTINAL	Chest pain associated with certain foods or medications, pain improves after taking an antacid	Pain in the upper right abdomen that can spread to the right shoulder blade or back, burning epigastric pain	*H. pylori* testing
MISCELLANEOUS	Chest pain associated with precipitating stressful events, recurrent somatic complaints, lightheadedness, and paresthesia	Chest pain associated with numbness, weakness, or vesicular rash	Test cluster of vesicles for herpes zoster and MRI of spine if chest pain is associated with numbness or weakness
CARDIAC: INFLAMMATORY	Sharp chest pain, palpitations, and shortness of breath	Listen for murmur or arrhythmias	CXR, ECG, and ECHO

SYSTEM	SIGNS/SYMPTOMS/HX	PHYSICAL EXAM	LABS/IMAGING
CARDIAC: INCREASED MYOCARDIAL DEMAND OR DECREASED SUPPLY	Family history of genetic or connective tissue disorders (Marfan Syndrome) and palpitations	Heart murmur or arrhythmias	CXR, ECG, and ECHO
CARDIAC: CORONARY ARTERIES ABNORMALITIES	Chest pain with history of Kawasaki disease, COVID-19, coronary vasculopathy in heart transplant patients		CXR, ECG, and ECHO
CARDIAC: MISCELLANEOUS	Sudden severe, sharp pain in chest or upper back	Heart murmur, low blood pressure, rapid weak pulse	CXR, ECG, and ECHO
CARDIAC: DRUGS	Chest pain with tobacco smokers, cocaine, and other sympathomimetic drugs	Vasoconstrictor activity of drugs lead to myocardial ischemia	CXR, ECG, and ECHO

IMAGING PEARLS

- **CHEST RADIOGRAPHY (CXR)** is used to look for cardiomegaly, bony lesions, airway obstruction, lung parenchymal disease, and pleural lesions.
- **ECG** is used to look at heart rate, rhythm, signs of ischemia, pericarditis, or chamber hypertrophy.
- **ECHOCARDIOGRAM** is used to look for abnormal cardiac anatomy, valvular dysfunction, coronary abnormalities, evidence of pericardial effusions, hypertrophy, and pulmonary hypertension.

DIFFERENTIAL DIAGNOSIS - NON-CARDIAC CHEST PAIN

MUSCULOSKELETAL

- **COSTOCHONDRITIS**: Look for inflammation of the costochondral joint in an older child. Pain worsens with movement and deep breaths.
- **TIETZE SYNDROME**: Usually found in a younger child with no history of trauma. Characterized by chest pain and swelling at the costochondral joint.
- **SLIPPING RIB SYNDROME**: Look for pain in the lower chest or upper abdomen due to hypermobility of the lower ribs.

- **TRAUMA/MUSCLE STRAIN/OVERUSE INJURY**: Look for a history of trauma or lifting heavy weights.
- **XIPHOID PAIN (XIPHOIDALGIA)**: Look for pain and tenderness at the xiphoid. Pain is worse with chest movement, bending, and lifting heavy objects.
- **SICKLE CELL VASO-OCCLUSIVE CRISIS**: Look for a person with sickle cell disease who is dehydrated or has a change in body temperature (fever or being outside in the cold) with acute chest pain.
- **NONSPECIFIC/IDIOPATHIC**

PULMONARY

- **BRONCHIAL ASTHMA**: Look for wheezing, increased work of breathing on exam, or nighttime cough.
- **EXERCISE-INDUCED/COUGH VARIANT ASTHMA**: Look for wheezing with, or after, exercise.
- **BRONCHITIS**: Look for fever, increased work of breathing, and possible hypoxia. Exam may reveal wheezes, crackles, and/or rhonchi.
- **PLEURISY**: Usually associated with a viral infection and sharp pain with deep inspiration.
- **PNEUMONIA**: Look for fever, increased work of breathing, hypoxia, and exam will show wheezes, crackles, and/or rhonchi.
- **PNEUMOTHORAX**: Look for a sudden onset of dyspnea. This can occur with asthma, cystic fibrosis, whooping cough, or after trauma. Check for a pneumothorax on x-ray. With a tension pneumothorax (typically after penetrating trauma), breath sounds are absent on the affected side and the trachea deviates away from the affected side due to a one-way valve effect.
- **PULMONARY EMBOLISM**: Associated with a hypercoagulable state or hereditary thrombophilias (such as factor V Leiden). Often associated with a deep vein thrombosis and severe sudden chest pain and dyspnea.
- **ACUTE CHEST SYNDROME**: This is a potentially fatal complication of sickle cell disease and is accompanied by fever, respiratory symptoms, and a new radiodensity on chest x-ray.

GASTROINTESTINAL

- **GERD**: Often seen after eating fatty, greasy, spicy, or acidic foods. Look for "wet burps," halitosis, and chest pain. Pain temporarily disappears with an antacid.
- **ESOPHAGEAL SPASM**: Look for painful muscle contractions in the chest. Often associated with GERD, certain foods, food that is too hot or cold, anxiety, and depression.
- **PEPTIC ULCER DISEASE**: Look for burning chest pain that temporarily disappears with an antacid. Often caused by too many NASIDs or *H. Pylori* infection.
- **DRUG-INDUCED ESOPHAGITIS/GASTRITIS**: Certain drugs cause a direct toxic effect on the esophageal mucosa, including certain antibiotics (doxycycline, clindamycin, amoxicillin, metronidazole, ciprofloxacin, and rifaximin), NSAIDs, aspirin, acetaminophen, warfarin, ascorbic acid, bisphosphonates, and chemotherapy/thoracic irradiation regimens.
- **CHOLECYSTITIS**: Inflammation of the gallbladder with pain in the upper right abdomen that can spread to the right shoulder blade or back. Pain can increase at approximately 20 minutes after eating.

MISCELLANEOUS

- **PANIC DISORDER**: Often associated with precipitating events and sudden onset.

- **HYPERVENTILATION**: May lead to musculoskeletal chest pain with strain or spasm of the intercostal chest wall muscles.
- **BREAST-RELATED CONDITIONS**: Mastalgia in females causes sharp breast pain and can be associated with the menstrual cycle.
- **HERPES ZOSTER**: Look for burning pain over the chest associated withing one dermatome (T1→T9) and a rash.
- **PSYCHOGENIC**: Look for recurrent somatic complaints (headaches, abdominal pain, or extremity pain).
- **SPINAL CORD/NERVE ROOT COMPRESSION**: Look for chest pain associated with numbness or weakness.

DIFFERENTIAL DIAGNOSIS – CARDIAC CHEST PAIN

INFLAMMATORY
- **PERICARDITIS**: Caused by inflammation of the heart lining. Look for sharp chest pain, palpitations, and shortness of breath. Associated with postpericardiotomy syndrome, systemic lupus erythematosus (SLE), Crohn's disease, and other autoimmune diseases. Caused by viruses (Coxsackie B, adenovirus, Hepatitis C, CMV, echovirus, influenza, EBV, and parvovirus B19) and bacteria (Staphylococcus, Streptococcus, Pneumococcus). Sometiems a friction rub can be heard on exam when the patient leans forward.
- **MYOCARDITIS**: Caused by inflammation of the heart muscle. Look for acute chest pain, shortness of breath, and arrhythmias. Caused by viruses (coxsackievirus B, adenovirus, hepatitis C, CMV, echovirus, influenza, EBV, and parvovirus B19) or bacteria (Staphylococcus, Streptococcus, Diphtheria, and Borrelia burgdorferi from Lyme Disease).

INCREASED MYOCARDIAL DEMAND OR DECREASED SUPPLY
- **CARDIOMYOPATHY**: May be dilated or hypertrophic. Look for chest pain with family history of genetic or connective tissue disorders (Marfan Syndrome).
- **LEFT VENTRICULAR OUTFLOW TRACT (LVOT) OBSTRUCTION**: Look for aortic stenosis, subaortic stenosis, or supravalvular aortic stenosis on echocardiogram.
- **ARRHYTHMIAS**: Look for chest pain with palpitations.

CORONARY ARTERY ABNORMALITIES
- **CONGENITAL CORONARY ARTERY ABNORMALITIES**: Anomalous Left Coronary Artery from Pulmonary Artery (ALCAPA), Anomalous Left Coronary Artery (ALCA) from right coronary sinus, and coronary fistula are some coronary artery anomalies. Chest x-ray may show an enlarged heart. Echocardiogram may provide a more definitive diagnosis, while cardiac catheterization will provide a definitive diagnosis.
- **ACQUIRED CORONARY ARTERY ABNORMALITIES**: Such anomalies may occur in Kawasaki disease, postsurgical situations (after arterial switch operation, after Ross procedure), and due to posttransplant coronary vasculopathy.

DRUGS
- **COCAINE, MARIJUANA, METHAMPHETAMINES, AND SYMPATHOMIMETIC DECONGESTANTS**: Look for chest pain in a patient using drugs that can cause vasoconstriction.

MISCELLANEOUS

- **AORTIC DISSECTION**: Look for sudden, severe, sharp pain in the chest or upper back, diastolic heart murmur, low blood pressure, rapid weak pulse, heavy sweating, or loss of vision.
- **RUPTURE OF AORTIC ANEURYSM**: Look for deep, constant pain in the abdomen and back, positive pulse near the umbilicus, hypotension, or loss of consciousness.
- **PULMONARY HYPERTENSION**: Look for chest pain, fatigue, shortness of breath, syncope, lower extremity edema, or heart palpitations.
- **MITRAL VALVE PROLAPSE**: Look for palpitations, arrhythmias, or shortness of breath with a heart murmur and a systolic click.
- **ATRIAL MYXOMAS**: These are non-cancerous tumors resulting in breathing difficulty, chest pain, or chest tightness.
- **CARDIAC DEVICE/STENT COMPLICATIONS**: Look for sudden chest pain after a cardiac procedure.

REFERENCES

https://www.uptodate.com/contents/causes-of-nontraumatic-chest-pain-in-children-and-adolescents
https://publications.aap.org/pediatricsinreview/article-abstract/31/1/e1/33227

Topic 9: Childhood-Onset Fluency Disorder – Providing Counseling
Provide counseling regarding childhood-onset fluency disorder

BACKGROUND
Developmental language disorders are very common. They occur in 5-10% of children. **Fluency disorders are developmental language disorders that result in the interruption of the flow of speech.** This may be in the form of an atypical rate, unusual rhythm, repetition of sounds, repetition of words, repetition of syllables, prolongation of sounds, sound blocks, speaking avoidance, and secondary mannerisms.

Speech fluency disorders can have significant **social, emotional, psychological, and functional impacts**. Before school entry, pediatricians may be the only professionals to assess the child, and so have an important role in screening for these relatively common developmental delays.

COMMON FLUENCY DISORDERS
Stuttering is the most common fluency disorder and is characterized by repetitions (e.g., sounds, syllables, words), prolongations of consonants (e.g., being ssssstuck on an "s"), and blocks (e.g., silent letters, or being unable to produce a letter). Stuttering is usually associated with significant tension in the speaker. Onset is usually around age 4 - 5 years. Stuttering is present in about 1% of school-aged children and is 3 times more common in boys. **Comorbid conditions may exist**, such as ADHD, seizure disorders, social anxiety disorders, and autism. Neurogenic stuttering results from disease or trauma.

Cluttering is another fluency disorder. In cluttering, the listener may hear speech that is rapid in pace, comes in spurts, has excessive breaks in the flow, sounds disorganized, or sounds like the speaker is unsure of what he/she/they want(s) to say. Patients with cluttering are often unaware that their message did not come across as intended, and therefore they may not attempt to fix the communication breakdown. **Comorbid conditions may exist**, such as a ADHD, learning disabilities, Tourette's, and autism.

PROVIDING COUNSELING
Counsel families to provide a **language-rich environment** which includes reading to their child. Infants and young children benefit from reciprocal interactions with adults and other children. Screen time is not a substitute. **Parent/caregiver and family involvement is essential** in the treatment of fluency disorders.

If a fluency disorder is suspected, and then confirmed by a speech-language pathologist, let families know that **early intervention is key**, and has the potential to affect educational and health outcomes.

Reassure parents/caregivers that **the vast majority of patients with fluency disorders will recover in childhood (about 90%).**

The **treatment process typically involves direct therapy with the child, and indirect work with the family** to help the family make changes as needed in the child's environment. Periodic re-evaluations to monitor progress may be necessary and beneficial.

Provide information about fluency disorders, including information from supportive 3rd party educators/supporters, such as:

- www.stutteringhelp.org
- FRIENDS: The National Association of Young People Who Stutter
- SAY: The Stuttering Association for the Young

Inform parents that evidence of the benefit of medications is mixed. Medications such as risperidone and olanzapine that block dopamine receptors (risperidone, olanzapine) have shown some benefit, but results have been difficult to replicate in subsequent studies.

Let parents/caregivers know that students with fluency disorders **may be eligible for accommodations in school**.

When appropriate, counsel parents concerned for stuttering in their child that this can be a normal developmental stage occurring between the age of 2 and 3, during which a phrase, or a word, or even a part of a word may be repeated. This typical developmental disfluency usually resolves by age 4.

REFERENCES
https://www.asha.org/practice-portal/clinical-topics/fluency-disorders
https://www.uptodate.com/contents/specific-learning-disabilities-in-children-role-of-the-primary-care-provider
https://www.uptodate.com/contents/etiology-of-speech-and-language-disorders-in-children
https://www.uptodate.com/contents/evaluation-of-speech-and-language-disorders-in-children
https://publications.aap.org/pediatrics/article/149/1%20Meeting%20Abstracts%20February%202022/52/185746/Childhood-onset-Fluency-Disorder-Stuttering-wait
Perez HR, Stoeckle JH. Stuttering; Clinical and research update. Can Fam Physician. 2016 Jun; 62(6): 479–484.

Topic 10: Children Behind on Vaccines or Having an Unknown Vaccination Record – Managing

Manage children who are behind on vaccines or have an unknown vaccination record

BACKGROUND

Vaccines, when given according to the standard vaccine schedule, protect patients by providing them with long-lasting immunity before they acquire disease. Vaccines also protect unimmunized persons through "herd" immunity.

The standard vaccine schedule can be reviewed on the CDC website here: https://www.cdc.gov/vaccines/schedules/hcp/imz/child-adolescent.html.

Recommendations for catch-up immunization schedules can be viewed here: https://www.cdc.gov/vaccines/schedules/hcp/imz/catchup.html.

CATCH-UP SCHEDULE

Use the minimum recommended intervals between doses for children who are behind on vaccines. If a vaccine series was started but not completed, it is **not necessary to restart the series**. On the CDC's catch-up vaccination site, tables are available which give guidance on catch-up schedules. In each table, start with the patient's age and the timing of previous documented vaccine doses, and then follow the recommendations for that particular patient's vaccine history. **The tables on the CDC website provide the most-detailed resource**, but general information about particular vaccine catch-up rules is provided below.

PNEUMOCOCCAL CONJUGATE VACCINE

The minimum interval between vaccines in this series is 4 weeks. If 1 or more doses were given at 12 months of age or older, no additional doses are needed. There is an online tool provided by the CDC which can create customized vaccine schedules for this vaccine series here: https://www2a.cdc.gov/vaccines/m/pneumo/pneumo.html.

HAEMOPHILUS INFLUENZAE TYPE B (HIB)

The minimum interval is 4 weeks between doses. At least one dose must be given after 12 months of age.

DIPHTHERIA, TETANUS, AND PERTUSSIS-CONTAINING VACCINES

The minimum interval is 4 weeks between doses for most doses. Dose 4 must be given at least 6 months after Dose 3, and Dose 5 must be given at least 6 months after dose 4 and at age 4 - 6 years. Tdap is given at 11 - 12 years.

INACTIVATED POLIO VACCINE

The minimum interval between doses is 4 weeks, except for the final dose, which should be given at least 6 months after the previous dose.

UNKNOWN VACCINATION RECORD

The CDC generally recommends **revaccination** if there are no vaccine records available, but using **serologic testing** for the presence of antibodies to vaccine-preventable illness is also a reasonable approach. Protective antibody levels are > 0.10 IU/mL.

Testing in children 5 months or older:
- Diphtheria antibody (IgG)
- Tetanus antibody (IgG)
- hepatitis B surface antibody (IgG)
- *H. influenzae* type b antibody (IgG)

Testing in children 12 months or older:
- Rubeola antibody (IgG)
- Mumps antibody (IgG)
- Rubella antibody (IgG)
- Varicella antibody (IgG)
- Hepatitis A antibody (total or igG)

REFERENCES

https://www.cdc.gov/vaccines/schedules/hcp/imz/catchup.html

https://publications.aap.org/pediatricsinreview/article-abstract/36/6/249/34873/Immunizations-Vaccinations-in-General

https://www.uptodate.com/contents/standard-immunizations-for-children-and-adolescents-overview

Topic 11: Chronic Illness in the Adolescent/Young Adult – Planning the Transition to an Adult Care Provider

Plan the transition to an adult care provider for an adolescent/young adult with chronic illness

BACKGROUND
For adolescents and young adults with chronic disease, transition of care from pediatric physicians and care teams to adult physicians and care teams is a challenging time. **The patient must successfully navigate from a pediatric to an adult-centered care model. Extra support is necessary.**

Adolescents and young adults benefit from a structured approach to this transition. **Unsuccessful transitions may lead to gaps in care, higher frequency of emergency department visits or inpatient stays, and further complications from their chronic disease.** A very helpful resource developed in part by the AAP for patients, families, and care providers is available at https://gottransition.org.

TRANSITION OF CARE PHASES
Begin preparations at least a year before the transfer of care for greatest success. A successful health care transition involves **three phases**:
- Transition preparation
- Transfer
- Adult care integration

TRANSITION PREPARATION – TIMING & TOOLS TO ASSESS READINESS
Depending on the specialty, the preparation may begin as early as age 12, but at a minimum should start about a year prior to the transfer. **Each institution should create a policy** regarding care transitions. A standard **scorable assessment tool should be used to check the patient's readiness** for transition. Education about disease self-management and about appropriate use of health care should be provided. **Progress toward transition readiness should be periodically re-assessed and tracked. Conversations about assent and consent are important** during this stage. Parents and caregivers should be gradually less involved during the medical visits but continue to supervise medications and health care at home. Transition of care documents should be prepared.

TRANSFER
Ideally, there should be a **gap of less than six months** between the last appointment with the pediatric care team and the first appointment with the adult team. **Documents** including the final transition readiness assessment and an updated plan of care should be available. The **pediatrician and pediatric subspecialists should be available for questions** from the adult physicians and care team.

ADULT CARE INTEGRATION
The adult team should develop a plan to welcome young adults to the new practice. At the first clinic visit, the team should **describe their practice and their approach to adult care**. Providers should **assess the young adult's self-care skills**. Physicians should ask about the young adult's health **priorities and goals**. The medical summary and plan of care should be updated. The adult practice should **communicate with the pediatric care team that the transfer occurred**. At future visits, support for ongoing development of self-care knowledge and skills should be provided.

REFERENCES

https://gottransition.org

https://www.jahonline.org/article/1054-139X(93)90143-D/pdf

https://www.degruyter.com/document/doi/10.1515/jtm-2020-0001/html

https://www.uptodate.com/contents/sickle-cell-disease-scd-in-adolescents-and-young-adults-aya-transition-from-pediatric-to-adult-care

Topic 12: Common Neonatal Birth Injuries – Recognizing and Managing
Recognize and manage common neonatal birth injuries

BACKGROUND
Birth injuries range from minor (e.g., laceration or bruising) to severe (e.g., such as spinal cord injuries). Injuries may **occur during labor, delivery, or after delivery** (e.g., during resuscitation). **Risk factors for neonatal birth injuries include** fetal macrosomia, maternal obesity, maternal pelvic anomalies, precipitous delivery, and any fetal presentation other than vertex position. The use of **forceps or a vacuum device** also increases the risk for neonatal birth injury.

BRACHIAL PLEXUS INJURIES

EVALUATION
These injuries are thought to be due to **stretching or traction, compression, or oxygen deprivation**. Lateral traction on the fetal head, typically in the setting of shoulder dystocia, is thought to be the most common cause. These injuries are diagnosed when **arm weakness (almost always unilateral)** in the brachial plexus nerve distribution is found at birth. There are several types of brachial plexus injuries.

Workup of these injuries includes obtaining a full history, focusing on risk factors and perinatal history. Physical exam should include testing reflexes, ROM testing, and observing spontaneous movements. An **asymmetric Moro reflex** is a red flag for brachial plexus injuries. Associated **fractures of the clavicle and humerus, plus subluxation of the shoulder** may occur, so radiological evaluation includes **x-rays and possible CT scans**.

ERB PALSY
Occurs due to a brachial plexus injury at C5–6 or –7 resulting in **paralysis of the upper arm (hand and wrist movements are unaffected)**. There is a "**waiter's tip**" configuration if C7 is involved. The **grasp and extension of the hand** are intact. **Respiratory distress can result** due to phrenic nerve injury (look for a broken clavicle) resulting in unilateral diaphragmatic paralysis. It is often associated with LGA babies, breech deliveries, and C-sections.
IMAGE: www.pbrlinks.com/ERBSPALSY1

KLUMPKE'S PALSY
Occurs due to brachial plexus injury at C8-T1. This affects the **lower arm and hand**. It carries a worse prognosis because the nerves are typically torn. It results in a **claw hand deformity** in which there is an **inability to grasp**. Horner's syndrome (below) may be present.
IMAGE: www.pbrlinks.com/ERBKLUMPKE (shows Erb's and Klumpke's)

ERB-KLUMPKE'S PALSY
Weakness in the arm and hand due to injury from C5 - T1, known as "flail arm." Horner syndrome may be present.

HORNER SYNDROME
Ptosis and miosis (C8-T1).
A T1 lesion results in **ptosis, miosis, and anhidrosis**. The affected eye has a droopy lid, a small pupil (anisocoria), and the eye is dry. Can be associated with Klumpke's Palsy.
IMAGE: www.pbrlinks.com/HORNERS1

MANAGEMENT
As soon as the diagnosis is suspected, patients should be **referred for physical and occupational therapy.** Therapy will focus on preventing contractures, including passive ROM exercises and perhaps splints. The **majority of infants with neurologic injury recover spontaneously. Surgery** (nerve transfers or soft tissue reconstruction of contractures) may be necessary if recovery does not occur in ~6 months.

SOFT TISSUE INJURIES

EVALUATION
These types of injuries include **swelling, bruising, petechiae, and perhaps lacerations** (in the case of C-section), and typically occur in the **presenting part of the infant's body**. Bruising and edema of the **genitalia** are frequently seen in breech presentation. Edema and petechiae of the **head and neck** are seen in vertex presentation, especially face presentation.

Subcutaneous fat necrosis usually occurs in the first few weeks of life. It is recognized by firm, indurated nodules (reddish, blue, or flesh colored) and plaques typically over bony prominences on the back, buttocks, limbs, or cheeks.

Lacerations typically occur with emergent C-sections, and occur on the presenting part of the infant's body, most often on the face or scalp.

MANAGEMENT
Bruising, edema, and petechiae are typically self-limiting and recover spontaneously. A **platelet count** may help in the evaluation of further development of petechiae or other areas of bleeding. **Bilirubin** levels should be monitored and hyperbilirubinemia treated in the case of **extensive bruising.** **Subcutaneous fat necrosis** is self-limiting and resolves over the course of several weeks, but is a **risk factor for hypercalcemia**. Monitor and treat as necessary. **Lacerations** typically only require steri-strips, rarely requiring plastic surgery.

EXTRACRANIAL INJURIES
Edema or hemorrhage into the various layers of scalp and skull are more likely after **prolonged labor or after instrumentation-assisted delivery**. Remember that the most superficial layer is the skin of the scalp with underlying fatty tissue. The next layer is the galea aponeurotica. Then comes the skull and periosteum. Further below is the dura mater, then arachnoid membrane closely adhered to the brain.

EVALUATION
CAPUT SUCCEDANEUM
Edema of the scalp, occasionally hemorrhagic, above the periosteum layer. This swelling **does cross suture lines**. Presents after prolonged labor due to pressure on the scalp, or after **vacuum extraction**.

CEPHALOHEMATOMAS

Rupture of small blood vessels between the periosteum and skull bone. This swelling **does not cross suture lines**. Much more likely if **forceps or vacuum** is used during delivery. CT or MRI will confirm subperiosteal location. Occasionally heals with calcifications, causing deformities of the skull. Suspect infection if the cephalohematoma starts to expand from its original size.

SUBGALEAL HEMORRHAGE

Accumulation of blood in the space between the galea aponeurotica and the periosteum, caused by damaged veins between the scalp and dural sinuses. This has the **potential for large blood losses and can be life-threatening**. This swelling **does cross suture lines, and may extend from forehead anteriorly to nape of the neck, and to the ears laterally**. The **swelling is fluctuant and may shift** with movement. Associated tachycardia and pallor may be observed, along with dropping hematocrit. Head US confirms the location of the hemorrhage.

MANAGEMENT

Caput succedaneum is typically benign and self-limited, resolving within a few days. Rarely, the lesion may become necrotic, leading to later scarring and alopecia.

Cephalohematomas are also typically self-resolved, but may take a few weeks to recover. These are associated with an **increased risk of hyperbilirubinemia**, sometimes severe. Bilirubin levels should be monitored closely. Potential complications of cephalohematomas include skull deformities from calcification, infection, and sepsis with E. coli.

Subgaleal hemorrhages can be severe and life-threatening. Early recognition of this diagnosis is key. Monitor vital signs frequently, as well as head circumference and hematocrit. CT or MRI helps to identify the location of the hemorrhage. Monitor CBC frequently, **treat with blood products, volume resuscitation**, and consider transfer to the ICU.

FRACTURES

EVALUATION
CLAVICULAR FRACTURES

Signs and symptoms may include lack of movement of the affected arm, asymmetric Moro reflex, crying with passive motion, edema, perhaps crepitus. Diagnosis is confirmed by X-ray of chest and upper extremities.

HUMERAL FRACTURES

Symptoms are similar to those listed above. There is crying with palpation and passive movement of the upper arm. Again, x-rays are helpful in making the diagnosis. MRI may be necessary if the fracture is very proximal or very distal, because of lack of ossification of the epiphysis.

FEMUR FRACTURES

There is an increased pain response with manipulation of the leg. There may be asymmetric movement of that leg and possible crepitus. X-ray of the affected leg confirms the diagnosis.

SKULL FRACTURES

These occur more frequently during forceps-associated delivery, but can occur in spontaneous vaginal delivery as well from pressure against maternal structures (sacral promontory or symphysis pubis). Premature infants are at increased risk. The skull fracture may be linear or depressed, and if occurring after forceps-associated delivery, are more likely to be associated with intracranial hemorrhage or cephalohematoma. Diagnosis is made by plain radiograph. CT may be necessary to assess intracranial bleeding.

MANAGEMENT

For most of these fractures, management is conservative. For clavicular and humeral fractures, the infant could be dressed in long sleeves, and the affected arm pinned to the chest with the elbow bent at a 90-degree angle. Femur fractures are treated with immobilization in a Pavlik harness for several weeks. Tylenol may be used for pain management. Repeat radiographs are helpful to document healing. Recognize that upper extremity fractures may be associated with brachial plexus injury. All fractures may be associated with diffuse osteoporosis or osteogenesis imperfecta. Cranial fractures may be associated with intracranial or extracranial hemorrhage.

REFERENCES

https://www.uptodate.com/contents/neonatal-birth-injuries
https://www.cureus.com/articles/10037

Topic 13: Common Pediatric Illnesses – Understanding and Applying Return-to-School Criteria

Understand and apply return-to-school criteria for common pediatric illnesses

BACKGROUND

School absences due to common illnesses may present a host of consequences. Parents may have to take time off from work, which can reduce the family's income and reduce productivity in the community. Children's educational needs may also be compromised. It is important to allow children to return to school as quickly as possible in a manner that is safe for the child with the illness and those at school who may be exposed to the child's illness.

COMMON ILLNESSES AND APPLYING RETURN TO SCHOOL CRITERIA

COMMON COLD

These are due to viral infections of the upper respiratory tract, most frequently being caused by Rhinovirus. They will typically present with cough, runny/stuffy nose, and/or pharyngitis. Children may return to school after **remaining afebrile for 24 hours without the need for fever reducing medications**.

INFLUENZA (aka "FLU")

The flu is caused by the influenza virus and typically presents with high fever, runny nose, pharyngitis, cough, headache, fatigue, and chills. Oseltamivir can reduce the duration of the illness if given early in the course. Children may return to school after **remaining afebrile for 24 hours without the need for fever reducing medications**.

BRONCHIOLITIS

Typically caused by a viral infection affecting the smallest airways in the lungs (the bronchioles). Most commonly caused by RSV and strongly associated with wheezing on exam. Patients also tend to have fever, rapid breathing, cough, and runny nose. Typically seen in children up to 2 years of age. May return to school or daycare once the **wheezing is gone and the child is afebrile for 24 hours without the need for fever reducing medications**.

OTITIS MEDIA

Inflammation of the middle ear often accompanied by a red, opaque, and bulging tympanic membrane. Most frequent pathogens are *Streptococcus pneumoniae, Haemophilus influenzae,* and *Moraxella catarrhalis*. **A child with otitis media only needs to stay home if:**

- The child has a fever. If so, the child may return to school once there is **no fever for 24 hours without the use of fever reducing medications**.
- The child is unable to participate due to **pain**.

STREP PHARYNGITIS

This is a bacterial infection of the throat caused by Group A Strep. Symptoms include pharyngitis, fever, headache, stomach pain/vomiting. Cough, runny nose, and diarrhea are not seen with Strep. Children can return to school after **fever is gone for 24 hours without the use of fever reducing medications and they have taken an antibiotic for at least 12 hours**.

ACUTE GASTROENTERITIS

This is typically caused by a viral infection. Symptoms can include vomiting, stomach pain, diarrhea, and fever. Kids can return to school **once the diarrhea is mild, they have control over loose stools, and fever has resolved for 24 hours without the need for fever reducing medications**.

LICE

Lice lay eggs (nits) which may be seen attached to hair. Itching is the main symptom. Spread of lice occurs primarily from direct hair-to-hair contact but may also occur through the sharing of clothes. Children should avoid contact with others until the first anti-lice treatment is done, but **my remain in school until the end of the school day** and do not need to be sent home early. **Treatment my begin in the evening and the child may return to school the next day. Nits may persist after treatment but do not spread lice and should not be a reason to send children home.**

HAND FOOT AND MOUTH DISEASE

This viral infection is caused by the Coxsackie virus. Symptoms include small, red spots and blisters on the palms, fingers, soles, and toes. Painful ulcers (sores) may also be present in the mouth. Rash can spread up arms, legs, and buttocks. Low grade fever is also common. **When the rash is severe and widespread children may need to stay home until the blisters dry up (which can take 7-10 days). Generally, children can return to school after the fever is gone without the use of fever reducing medication and there is no drooling in the presence of ongoing mouth sores.**

CONJUNCTIVITIS

Not all red eyes are due to an infectious etiology. When due to an infection, the most common etiology is a virus. Viral conjunctivitis is typically associated with serous or mucoid discharge, while bacterial conjunctivitis is associated with purulent discharge. Bacterial conjunctivitis should be treated with antibiotic eye drops, but the child can return to school. Children with "pink eye" **do not need to miss school if they have been afebrile for 24 hours without fever reducing medications.**

REFERENCES
https://www.cdc.gov/hand-foot-mouth/about/prevention.html
https://www.cdc.gov/conjunctivitis/about/transmission.html
https://www.afterhourspediatrics.com/resources/what-to-know-rsv
https://www.cdc.gov/flu/school/guidance.htm
https://www.cdc.gov/parasites/lice/head/parents.html
https://www.cdc.gov/dotw/strepthroat/index.html

Topic 14: Common Viral Exanthems – Recognizing
Recognize common viral exanthems

BACKGROUND
A viral exanthem is an eruptive skin rash associated with a viral infection. These are common in childhood, however, immunizations against measles, mumps, rubella, and chickenpox have greatly reduced the burden of disease. Some common childhood viral exanthems are varicella, fifth disease (parvovirus B19), measles, roseola, and rubella. **Many viral exanthems have distinct patterns.**

MEASLES (AKA RUBEOLA)
The three C's of "**COUGH**, **CONJUNCTIVITIS**, and **CORYZA**" are the classic symptoms of measles (AKA rubeola). Coryza refers to rhinorrhea. Also look in the mouth for KOPLIK SPOTS and on the skin for a rash. **The three C's come first, then the Koplik spots, and the LAST symptom to appear is the RASH.** The rash **starts at the head (around the hairline) and progresses down**. The rash resolves after about 5 days. Patients are extremely contagious from four days prior to the onset of the rash until four days after the rash appears and require negative pressure isolation when hospitalized.
- **IMAGE**: www.pbrlinks.com/koplik (Koplik Spots)
- **IMAGE**: www.pbrlinks.com/measles-rash (Measles Rash)

RUBELLA VIRUS (AKA GERMAN MEASLES)
In children, the Rubella virus causes "German measles" and presents with a mild fever and a **maculopapular rash. The rash starts on the face and then spreads to the trunk and extremities within 24 hours. The facial rash starts to disappear as the body rash starts**. The rash resolves within 3 days. In unimmunized children who get this infection, it's generally a benign, self-limited viral illness. If contracted during the first trimester of pregnancy, look for signs of congenital rubella.
- **IMAGE**: www.pbrlinks.com/rubella

VARICELLA ZOSTER VIRUS (CHICKEN POX)
The varicella zoster virus causes chicken pox. Lesions may be **described as a "dew drop on a petal"** during the vesicle phase. Lesions are said to **come in "crops" at different times, and will therefore appear in different stages on the body (some vesicles, some crusted lesions)**. The rash starts at the **trunk and then spreads to the face and extremities**. It lasts for 7–10 days and leaves minimal scars.
- **IMAGE**: www.pbrlinks.com/varicella

HUMAN HERPES VIRUS 6 (AKA HHV-6)
Human herpes virus 6 (AKA HHV-6) **causes roseola**. Look for a child **6 months to 2 years of age with sudden onset of high fever**. The patient **may have neurological symptoms including seizure or encephalopathy**. The key is to look for a **rash a few days after the fever subsides**. The rash is usually on the **neck, trunk, and thighs**. Children may return to school after the fever is gone, even with the rash!
- **MNEMONIC**: Look for an infant or toddler who feels and looks like a ½ DOZEN (6) ROSY ROSES. Well, of course she does now that the FEVER'S GONE and the patient finally presents to the doc!
- **IMAGE**: www.pbrlinks.com/HHV1

ERYTHEMA INFECTIOSUM
This rash is caused by Parvovirus B19 and is also called fifth disease. Look for **erythematous facial flushing of the cheeks (sometimes described as "slapped cheeks" appearance). The extremities will**

have diffuse macular (or morbilliform) erythema (especially on the extensor surfaces) referred to as "lacy" or "reticular." Diagnose with IgM titers.

- **PEARLS**: The **rash occurs AFTER the slapped cheeks rash** (often a week later). Patients may also have knee or ankle pain. Parvovirus B19 infection can result in aplastic crisis. Intrauterine exposure can result in hydrops fetalis.
- **MNEMONIC**: infectio5uM = FIFTH disease = "Fiver fingers." Imagine a cheek being SLAPPED with FIVE fingers covered by a white LACY glove with a red M on the back of it (extensor surface). M = IgM titers.
  - **IMAGE**: www.pbrlinks.com/slapped-cheeks
  - **IMAGE**: www.pbrlinks.com/infectiousum

HERPES SIMPLEX VIRUS (HSV)

The initial flare for this STD is often very painful. Pain may precede the presentation of lesions. **Look for multiple, painful ulcers or vesicles on the labia or penis**. The patient can have lymphadenopathy. The **vesicles are clustered on an erythematous base, but lesions can also be ulcerative**. Diagnose by obtaining HSV PCR or a viral culture. The Tzanck smear is not specific for HSV.

- **IMAGE**: www.pbrlinks.com/HSV1
- **IMAGE**: www.pbrlinks.com/HSV2

COXSACKIE VIRUS & ENTEROVIRUS

Coxsackie virus is a subtype of the Enterovirus family and both can cause **hand, foot, and mouth disease**. Look for a **fever, sore throat, and a maculopapular and vesicular rash on the palms and soles. Also look for small white lesions at the posterior oropharynx or ulcers on the tongue**. Some patients only have oral lesions. The **skin lesions can be very tender**. Can give steroids for severe pain.

- **PEARL**: If present, the oral lesions actually appear first! Maybe it should be called mouth, hand, and foot disease!
- **IMAGE**: www.pbrlinks.com/COXSACKIEVIRUS1
- **IMAGE**: www.pbrlinks.com/COXSACKIEVIRUS2
- **IMAGE**: www.pbrlinks.com/COXSACKIEVIRUS3
- **MNEMONIC**: MOUTH, HAND, AND FOOT DISEASE! Imagine the hands and feet being fine until AFTER the kid sticks them in his INFECTIOUS MOUTH!

GIANOTTI-CROSTI SYNDROME (GCS) (AKA PAPULAR ACRODERMATITIS)

Look for a viral infection preceding a child between the ages of **9 months and 9 years of age with a symmetric, skin-colored papules or papulovesicles that possibly coalesces into plaques involving the** cheeks, buttocks, and extensor surfaces of the forearms, legs, and feet. It can be pruritic or asymptomatic. Often triggered by a viral infection.

- **PEARL**: Can develop petechial or purpural lesions with hepatitis B virus infection
- **PEARL**: Other associated viruses include EBV, CMV, enterovirus, echoviruses, RSV, and SARS-CoV-2 (COVID-19)
- **PEARL**: Does not cause mucosal lesions. Often resolve spontaneously within two months.
- **IMAGE**: www.pbrlinks.com/acrodermatitis

ERYTHEMA NODOSUM

For erythema nodosum, look for **painful, shiny, red to bluish skin lesions in a patient with a history of a chronic disease or on certain medications**. Associations include Crohn's Disease, Ulcerative Colitis, Drugs (oral contraceptives and sulfa drugs), Infections (Yersinia, EBV, Tuberculosis, fungal infections), and Sarcoidosis.

- **IMAGE**: www.pbrlinks.com/ERYTHEMA-N1
- **IMAGE**: www.pbrlinks.com/ERYTHEMA-N2
- **IMAGE**: www.pbrlinks.com/ERYTHEMA-N3

REFERENCE
https://www.medscape.com/viewarticle/734882

Topic 15: Conjunctivitis in Patients – Evaluating and Managing
Evaluate and manage a patient with conjunctivitis

BACKGROUND
Conjunctivitis is one of the most common nontraumatic eye complaints. The common etiologies include infections (viral or bacterial) and allergies.

EVALUATING CONJUNCTIVITIS
Bilateral disease is often allergic, whereas unilateral disease suggests a viral, bacterial, chemical, mechanical, or lacrimal origin.

BACTERIAL
Bacterial conjunctivitis is characterized by acute onset with minimal pain, some pruritus, and often exposure history (daycare or school). Exam will show a purulent (yellow, white, or green) discharge that recurs at lid margins and corners of eye after wiping lids. The conjunctiva often has a pink or red appearance. Bacterial conjunctivitis is usually unilateral but may become bilateral. The combination of the following 4 clinical features results in a likely **negative bacterial conjunctival culture**:

- Age 6 years or older
- Presentation in April-November
- Discharge that is absent or watery
- Lack of a "glued eye" in the morning

VIRAL
Viral conjunctivitis can have acute or subacute onset with pruritus, minimal pain, and often exposure history (daycare or school). It is often associated with a viral prodrome (fever, adenopathy, pharyngitis, or other URI symptoms). Exam will show watery with strands of mucous discharge with grittiness, burning, or irritation of eyes. Viral conjunctivitis usually starts as a unilateral process but commonly spreads to become a bilateral conjunctivitis. The conjunctiva is often pink or red with a bumpy appearance.

ALLERGIC
Allergic conjunctivitis can have an acute or subacute onset with no pain or infectious exposure history. Pruritis is extremely common and clear watery discharge from the eye is seen. This typically presents as a bilateral conjunctivitis. Often associated with nasal congestion, sneezing, and wheezing. Exam will show irritated eyes with grittiness and burning sensations. The conjunctiva are pink, puffy, and bumpy appearing.

MANAGING CONJUNCTIVITIS
When it comes to managing conjunctivitis, it depends on the etiology.

BACTERIAL
Most cases of bacterial conjunctivitis are self-limiting. However, you can treat with topical antibiotics such as **erythromycin ophthalmic ointment** or **trimethoprim-polymyxin B drops** as they may shorten symptoms duration of the illness and limit transmission to other people. Educate the patient regarding careful and frequent hand washing to reduce transmission to the other eye and to other people.

VIRAL

Treat viral conjunctivitis symptoms with **decongestants or ophthalmic topical antihistamines** such as olopatadine, ketotifen and naphazoline-pheniramine. Also, a warm/cool compresses and lubricating drops can provide symptomatic relief for viral conjunctivitis. Educate the patient regarding careful and frequent hand washing to reduce transmission to the other eye and to other people.

ALLERGIC

Treatment goals for allergic conjunctivitis are to minimize exposure to allergens. Topical lubricants and cool compress can provide symptomatic relief and comfort. **Topical ophthalmic antihistamines** (olopatadine, ketotifen and naphazoline-pheniramine) or **systemic antihistamines** can also improve symptoms for more severe cases.

RETURN TO SCHOOL, WORK, OR SPORTS

VIRAL CONJUNCTIVITIS

Viral conjunctivitis is usually self-limited to 10-14 days, but symptoms may persist for as many as 6 weeks. These patients may be allowed to return to school if they are **afebrile for 24 hours without fever-reducing medications** and are able to avoid close contact with others.

ALLERGIC CONJUNCTIVITIS

Allergic conjunctivitis is not contagious and therefore **does not require any special precautions** to return to school/work. For any type of conjunctivitis, it is important for a child to be seeing clearly before returning to play.

BACTERIAL CONJUNTIVITIS

SCHOOL/WORK

These patients may be allowed to return to school if they are **afebrile for 24 hours without fever-reducing medications** and are able to avoid close contact with others. Many daycares/schools, however, require resolution of purulent discharge and at least 24 hours of topical antibiotic therapy prior to return.

SPORTS

Patients may return when **seeing clearly** and have used topical antibiotic therapy for at least 24 hours with resolution of purulent eye drainage.

URGENT OPHTHALMOLOGIC REFERRAL

If any of the following symptoms are noted, it is important to make an urgent ophthalmologic referral because the following signs and symptoms can be associated with conditions that can lead to blindness.

SYMPTOMS	DIAGNOSIS
Photophobia	Infectious keratitis, iritis, or angle-closure glaucoma
Ciliary flush (Injection of deep conjunctiva and/or injection of episcleral vessels around the cornea	Infectious keratitis, iritis, or angle-closure glaucoma
Severe foreign body sensation	Infectious keratitis
Corneal opacity	Infectious keratitis
Fixed pupil	Angle-closure glaucoma
Severe headache with nausea	Angle-closure glaucoma
Loss of visual acuity	Infectious keratitis, iritis, or angle-closure glaucoma

REFERENCES

https://www.uptodate.com/contents/conjunctivitis
https://emedicine.medscape.com/article/797874-overview

Topic 16: Dysphagia – Diagnosing and Evaluating
Diagnose and evaluate dysphagia

BACKGROUND
Swallowing is a multi-step process by which a bolus of food is transferred from the mouth to the stomach. In the **oropharyngeal phase**, the bolus is transferred to the upper esophagus while the soft palate protects the nasal passage, and the epiglottis protects the airway. In the **esophageal phase**, the bolus is transferred through the esophagus to the stomach via esophageal peristalsis. **Disruption of either of these phases is termed "dysphagia," or difficulty swallowing. This is different than "odynophagia,"** or pain with swallowing.

SIGNS AND SYMPTOMS - OROPHARYNGEAL VS ESOPHAGEAL DYSPHAGIA
In narrowing the differential, it may be helpful to consider the **nature of onset** (sudden CVA or foreign body ingestion vs. subacute infectious or autoinflammatory disease onset) and **speed of progression** (non-progressive developmental abnormality vs. a progressive compressive mass effect) of dysphagia. **Review of symptoms** (presence of fever, pain, mental status, muscle weakness outside of the GI tract, rashes), **current diagnoses** (example Crohn's disease in esophagus), and **current medication** list (example, candida in immunosuppression, or pill esophagitis) may also be informative.

Dysphagia to **both liquids and solids suggests dysmotility** (typically an esophageal issue), which dysphagia to **solids alone suggests a structural abnormality or mucosal disease**, which may be due to an esophageal or oropharyngeal issue.

OROPHARYNGEAL DYSPHAGIA
The following symptoms are **more consistent with disorders of the oropharynx** rather than the esophagus:
- Delayed swallow initiation
- Post-nasal regurgitation or cough with swallowing
- Drooling
- Throat clearing

ESOPHAGEAL DYSPHAGIA
The following symptoms are **more consistent with a disorder of the esophagus** rather than the oropharyngx:
- Retrosternal chest pain
- A "sticking" sensation during and after swallowing

DIFFERENTIAL DIAGNOSIS FOR OROPHARYNGEAL ETIOLOGIES
The differential diagnosis for dysphagia is broadly categorized into **structural causes, infectious/inflammatory mucosal disease, or neuromuscular/motility impairment**. Typically, structural causes are ruled out first prior to further investigations of mucosa or motility.

STRUCTURAL CAUSES
- Cleft lip or palate
- Goiter
- Lymphadenopathy (infectious, inflammatory, malignancy)

INFECTIOUS/INFLAMMATORY CONDITIONS
- Retropharyngeal/peritonsillar abscess
- Coxsackie, CMV/HSV, epiglottitis

NEUROMUSCULAR DISORDERS
- Guillain-Barré, Multiple sclerosis, Myasthenia gravis, Juvenile Dermatomyositis
- CNS tumor or Cerebrovascular accident
- Botulism or Tetanus
- Globus sensation

DIFFERENTIAL DIAGNOSIS FOR ESOPHAGEAL ETIOLOGIES

STRUCTURAL CAUSES
- Esophageal web, stricture, diverticulum, fistula, swallowed foreign body
- Mediastinal mass, vascular ring

INFECTIOUS/INFLAMMATORY CONDITIONS
- Pill esophagitis, caustic ingestion
- Candida, eosinophilic esophagitis, HSV
- GERD

MOTILITY DISORDERS
- Achalasia
- Scleroderma
- Diffuse esophageal spasm

EVALUATION OF DYSPHAGIA

Based on the **history and exam, clinical suspicion will drive further evaluation** when warranted. Often the **clinical scenario sufficiently narrows the differential diagnosis and extensive workup is not necessary.**

When investigation of dysphagia is needed, the workup will be dictated by the differential diagnosis, and may include **serum studies, radiographs, CT, MRI, and PET scans**. Some of the more general studies performed for dysphagia include:
- **FIBEROPTIC ENDOSCOPIC EVALUATION:** An otolaryngologist uses a fiberoptic scope to visually examine the structure of the oropharynx and appearance of the tissue. The physician may witness the coordination of the rise of the soft palate, protection of the larynx by the epiglottis and movement of the vocal cords.
- **VIDEOFLUOROSCOPIC BARIUM STUDIES:** The fluoroscopic swallow study (performed with a speech/occupational therapist present) and esophagram involves the **ingestion of barium and tracking through the oropharyngeal and esophageal phases. This may reveal** discoordinated aspiration of barium into the airway during the oropharyngeal phase of swallowing, or structural impediments to swallowing such as a foreign body, esophageal web, abnormal dilation or fistulizing tract.
- **UPPER ENDOSCOPY:** A gastroenterologist uses an endoscope with the capability to visually inspect and biopsy the mucosa of the esophagus, stomach, and duodenum in an

anesthetized patient. This may uncover infectious and inflammatory etiologies of esophageal dysphagia.

- **ESOPHAGEAL MANOMETRY**: A gastroenterologist places a manometry catheter in the esophagus in an awake patient who performs a series of swallowing maneuvers to investigate the neuromuscular integrity of the esophagus.

REFERENCE

Mazoff, E. "Focus on Diagnosis: Dysphagia." *Pediatrics in Review* (2012) 33 (11): 518–520.

Topic 17: Emergency Contraception in Adolescent Patients – Understanding Usage
Understand use of emergency contraception in adolescent patients

BACKGROUND

Emergency contraception can be used to **prevent pregnancy** after having **unprotected sex**. This would include sex without any contraceptive method and incorrect usage of contraception (e.g., condom breakage or missing OCP doses). Unprotected sex can be a result of forced sex from a sexual assault. The two types of emergency contraception include either an **oral medication** or an **intrauterine device (IUD)**. Emergency contraception **does not cause abortions** since it does not interfere with an existing pregnancy.

ORAL MEDICATIONS

ULIPRISTAL ACETATE (UPA)

UPA is an **FDA approved** emergency contraceptive **oral progesterone receptor agonist-antagonist**. It can be used **up to 120 hours after unprotected sex**. The patient's menstrual cycle may be **delayed** after taking UPA, therefore they should take a pregnancy test if a menstrual cycle does not occur within 3 weeks of taking UPA. UPA is only available with a **prescription**, but many pharmacies do not carry it. **Headache, nausea, and abdominal pain** are the most common side effects.

LEVONORGESTREL (LNG)

LNG is an **FDA approved** emergency contraceptive **oral progestin**. It can be used **up to 72 hours after unprotected sex**. The patient's menstrual cycle may occur **sooner** than expected after taking LNG. A pregnancy test should be taken if a menstrual cycle does not occur within 3 weeks of taking LNG. LNG is available **over the counter without a prescription**, but it can be **expensive** ($30 - $50). **Heavier menstrual bleeding and spotting** are the most common side effects.

YUZPE METHOD

The **Yuzpe method** is an **off-label use** of **combined oral contraceptive pills (OCPs)** in which the patient takes two doses of OCPs 12 hours apart. The pills should each contain at least 100 micrograms of ethinyl estradiol and at least 500 micrograms of levonorgestrel. **Nausea and vomiting** are the most common side effects, therefore **premedicating with an antiemetic may be helpful**.

INTRAUTERINE DEVICES (IUDs)

COPPER IUD (CU-IUD)

Cu-IUDs are the **most effective type of emergency contraception,** and they have the additional benefit of providing **maintenance contraception** after placement. They should be placed by a **trained professional within 5 days of unprotected sex**. Heavy menstrual bleeding and dysmenorrhea are the most common side effects. **Contraindications** for placement include **Wilson's Disease**, **active cervical/pelvic infections**, or **abnormal anatomy** that prevents insertion.

OTHER CLINICAL CONSIDERATIONS

AWARENESS AND ACCESS FOR ADOLESCENTS

Oral emergency contraceptives have **better efficacy** the **sooner they are taken**, but their efficacy may be **decreased** if the patient is **overweight**. **Cu-IUDs** have **similar efficacy** at any point prior to its time limit, and its efficacy is **not affected** by the patient's weight. **Hormonal IUDs have not been approved for emergency contraception.** Although research has shown that an already established pregnancy would not be affected by emergency contraception, **pregnancy is the only absolute contraindication for emergency contraceptive use**. Both male and female patients should be made aware of the availability and options of emergency contraceptives so they can discuss the option with their partner if the need arises.

INITIATING MAINTENANCE CONTRACEPTION AFTER STARTING EMERGENCY CONTRACEPTION
Maintenance hormonal contraception can be started, or resumed, **immediately** after starting **LNG** or the **Yuzpe method**, but it should be **delayed for 5 days** after starting **UPA** since it may interfere with UPA's mode of action. Due to the delay in ovulation after taking oral emergency contraceptives, abstinence or condom use should be advised for **at least 7 days** after starting maintenance hormonal contraception.

ASSESSING FOR STD RISKS
Patients should be reminded that emergency contraceptives **do not protect against STDs**. STD screening for gonorrhea and chlamydia is not needed prior to Cu-IUD insertion, but it can be done during placement if needed. **STD screening** and a **review of maintenance contraception** should be **recommended** for any patient visit for emergency contraception.

REFERENCES
https://www.uptodate.com/contents/emergency-contraception
https://publications.aap.org/pediatrics/article/144/6/e20193149/37988

Topic 18: Febrile Seizures – Understanding the Clinical Features, Management and Prognosis
Understand the clinical features, management and prognosis of febrile seizures

BACKGROUND
This is the most common neurologic disorder of infants and small children (2-4% of children) usually occurring from 6 months to 5 years of age.

CLINICAL FEATURES
Febrile seizures commonly occur on the first day of illness. Seizures occur as the temperature increases rapidly with most fevers measured > 39 degrees Celsius. There must be a documented fever at the time of seizure activity for it to be called a **febrile seizure**.

SIMPLE FEBRILE SEIZURE (80%)
These are **generalized seizures** that typically last less than 15 minutes. They **do not recur in a 24-hour period**. The mean duration is 3 to 4 minutes. They are typically tonic-clonic, but atonic and tonic spells can happen. The post-ictal phase is associated with confusion, agitation, and drowsiness, but children usually **return to baseline quickly**. A brief description of **generalized seizures** is listed below:
- Begins in both hemispheres of the brain at the same time
- Movements include atonic (loss of muscle tone), tonic (muscle contractions), or tonic-clonic (rhymical movements of tightening and loosening of muscle tone)
- Loss of consciousness

COMPLEX FEBRILE SEIZURE (20%)
These are **focal onset seizures** that typically **last more than 15 minutes**. They often are **recurrent within a 24-hour period**. These seizures are more common in young children with **abnormal development**. Most children develop complex febrile seizures with their first seizure (as opposed to having a simple febrile seizure now and then developing a complex febrile seizure later during the course of the illness). A brief description of **focal seizures** is listed below:
- No loss of consciousness
- Simple focal seizures (aka auras) affect one area of the brain and include motor (jerky movements), sensory (hearing problems, hallucinations, or olfactory symptoms), autonomic (change blood pressure, heart rhythm, or bowel/bladder function), and psychic (feelings of fear, anxiety, or déjà vu)
- Complex focal seizures often are preceded by simple focal seizure (aka aura) and result in a blank stare into space or automatisms (non-purposeful, repetitive movements like lip smacking, blinking, grunting, etc.)
- Focal seizures begin in one area of the brain and can become generalized and spread to other areas, at which loss of consciousness may occur.

FEBRILE STATUS EPILEPTICUS (<1%)
These are continuous seizures, or intermittent seizures without neurologic recovery, **lasting 30 minutes or longer**. Consider getting a lumbar puncture (LP) to rule out meningitis. A brief description of **status epilepticus** is listed below:
- Can be convulsive (jerking motions, grunting sounds, drooling, and rapid eye movements) or nonconvulsive (appear confused and unable to speak and behaving in an irrational way)

- If the eyes are persistently open and deviated to the side, then this is an ongoing focal seizure even if convulsive activity has stopped.

MANAGEMENT

EMERGENCY RESCUE THERAPY
Most resolve spontaneously by the time the child is evaluated in the ED. Treat the fever with antipyretics and discuss proper positioning with the child on its side during a seizure. If the febrile seizure lasts more than 5 minutes, then treat with **benzodiazepines** (diazepam or lorazepam). If there is no IV access, give **buccal midazolam** or **intranasal lorazepam**. Monitor the airway, respiratory status, and circulatory status.

FEBRILE STATUS EPILEPTICUS
Start with emergency rescue therapy above and if unable to stop the febrile seizure with benzodiazepines, then use additional antiepileptics such as **IV fosphenytoin** and admit to the PICU for close monitoring of airway, respiratory status, and circulatory status. Important signs that a seizure has ended include closed eyes and deep breathing.

PROGNOSIS
Simple febrile seizures a have good overall prognosis with a recurrence rate of only 30-35%. The use of antipyretics at the first sign of fever **does NOT prevent future febrile seizures**.

NEGATIVE NEUROLOGICAL OUTCOMES
Neurological disorders are unlikely to occur in children after a simple febrile seizure, however complex febrile seizures and febrile status epilepticus can lead to new neurologic deficits, intellectual impairment, and behavioral disorders.

SUBSEQUENT EPILEPSY
The epilepsy risk in children with a simple febrile seizure is 1-2%, which is slightly **higher than the general population**. The epilepsy risk for a child with a complex febrile seizure, abnormal developmental history, or a family history of epilepsy increases to 5-10%. **An electroencephalogram (EEG) is not routinely recommended after a simple febrile seizure.**

FEBRILE STATUS EPILEPTICUS
Febrile status epilepticus leads to an increased risk for recurrent febrile seizures as well as afebrile seizures (epilepsy).

REFERENCES:
https://www.uptodate.com/contents/clinical-features-and-evaluation-of-febrile-seizures
https://www.uptodate.com/contents/treatment-and-prognosis-of-febrile-seizures
https://publications.aap.org/pediatricsinreview/article/18/1/5/36682/Febrile-Seizures

Topic 19: Fetal Alcohol Spectrum Disorder – Understanding the Clinical Features, Approach to Evaluation, and Differential Diagnosis

Understand the clinical features, approach to evaluation, and differential diagnosis of fetal alcohol spectrum disorder

BACKGROUND

Alcohol is a teratogen and prenatal exposure can lead to **Fetal Alcohol Spectrum Disorder (FASD).** FASD describes the effects alcohol can have in patients who were exposed to alcohol prenatally, including their **physical, behavioral,** and **neurodevelopmental** features.

CLINICAL FEATURES

FACIAL DYSMORPHISM

The three most common facial characteristics of FASD include **short palpebral fissures**, a **smooth philtrum**, and a **thin vermillion border**.

Other possible facial features that can be seen, but are not part of the diagnostic criteria, are a hypoplastic midface, epicanthal folds, flat nasal bridge, long philtrum, decreased distance between pupils, anteverted nares, decreased intercanthal distance, and ptosis.

STRUCTURAL CONGENITAL ANOMALIES

CONGENITAL HEART DISEASE

Congenital heart disease is **more common** in children with FASD than the general population and can include defects such as:

- Atrial septal defect (ASD)
- Ventricular septal defect (VSD)
- Conotruncal defects (e.g., Tetralogy of Fallot)

MUSCULOSKELETAL DEFECTS

Musculoskeletal defects may include:

- **Camptodactyly** (bent finger that cannot be straightened)
- **Contractures** of large joints
- **Pectus excavatum**
- Scoliosis
- Hypoplastic nails
- Klippel-Feil Syndrome

RENAL ANOMALIES

Renal anomalies may include:

- Horseshoe kidney
- Aplastic kidney
- Dysplastic kidney
- Hypoplastic kidneys
- Hydronephrosis
- Ureteral duplications

OPHTHALMOLOGICAL ANOMALIES

Ophthalmological anomalies may include:

- **Ptosis**
- Strabismus
- Optic nerve hypoplasia

AUDITORY ANOMALIES

Auditory anomalies can be either conductive or sensorineural **hearing loss**.

CNS STRUCTURAL ANOMALIES

CENTRAL NERVOUS SYSTEM INVOLVEMENT

CNS structural anomalies may include:

- **Microcephaly**
- Abnormalities in the **shape or size of structures** including the cerebellum, corpus callosum, or basal ganglia can occur.

Additional CNS involvement **may present differently at different ages.**

- **INFANCY**: During infancy, it can present as:
  - **Delayed development**
  - **Irritability**
  - Issues regulating state (arousal, sleep, and attention)
  - Autonomic instability
  - Jitteriness
- **CHILDHOOD**: During **childhood**, it may present as:
  - **Behavioral problems**
  - **Cognitive impairment** (lower IQ)
  - **Learning disabilities**
  - **Hyperactivity**
  - **Inattention**
  - Emotional reactivity
  - impairments in vision or listening, hypotonia, and **seizures**.
  - Memory and reasoning deficits
- **ADOLESCENCE**: During **adolescence**, it may present as:
  - Issues with social skills
  - Deficits in adaptive or executive functioning

EVALUATION OF FASD

A **comprehensive and multidisciplinary** approach should be used to evaluate a patient suspected of having FASD by including a physician who is an expert such as a **pediatric neurologist**, a **geneticist**, or a **developmental-behavioral pediatrician**.

DIAGNOSTIC CRITERIA OF FASD

Although there is **no universally accepted diagnostic criteria for FASD**, the **most common** includes **prenatal exposure to alcohol** and two or three of the following:

- **Characteristic facial dysmorphia** (short palpebral fissures, thin vermillion border, or smooth philtrum)
- **CNS involvement** (structural, neurologic, or functional)
- **Growth retardation**

DIFFERENTIAL DIAGNOSIS OF FASD

DIAGNOSES WITH SIMILAR FACIAL FEATURES

Other genetic conditions can resemble the facial features of FASD. These conditions include **Williams Syndrome**, **Noonan Syndrome**, **Cornelia de Lange Syndrome**, **DiGeorge Syndrome**, fetal hydantoin syndrome, toluene embryopathy, fetal valproate syndrome, and the fetal effects of maternal PKU.

DIAGNOSES WITH GROWTH RETARDATION AND MICROCEPHALY

Prenatal and postnatal growth retardation and microcephaly can be due to many others causes, including **genetic or chromosomal abnormalities, metabolic disorders, fetal infections, and other teratogens**.

DIAGNOSES WITH SIMILAR NEUROBEHAVIORAL PROBLEMS

Neurobehavioral disorders can be due to diagnoses such as **ADHD**, **autism spectrum disorder**, **global developmental delay**, **mood disorders** (e.g., depression or bipolar disorder), **schizophrenia**, conduct disorder, oppositional defiant disorder, PTSD, sleep disorders, and substance abuse. **Environmental factors** can also play a role in causing neurobehavioral problems such as **child abuse or neglect**, **poverty**, **early adversity or trauma**, early loss, poor prenatal environment, and caregiver substance abuse.

REFERENCES

https://www.uptodate.com/contents/fetal-alcohol-spectrum-disorder-clinical-features-and-diagnosis

Topic 20: Generalizability of a Research Study – Understanding Influential Factors

Understand factors that influence generalizability of a research study

BACKGROUND

The concept of "generalizability of a research study" refers to the **ability of the results of a research study to be applied to individuals and circumstances beyond the study population**. Generalizability is important to consider in interpreting study so that it is only applied to certain populations. **If the generalizability of a study is low, this limits the number of populations the results can be applied to**.

INTERNAL vs EXTERNAL VALIDITY

Generalizability is synonymous with external validity.

Conversely, **internal validity** is the ability of a study to draw conclusions about the specific variables included in one particular study. Often **steps taken to improve internal validity narrow the study population** and circumstances and therefore reduce generalizability.

FACTORS THAT REDUCE GENERALIZABILITY

- Stringent eligibility criteria
- Highly controlled study conditions
- Selection or recruitment bias
- Randomized controlled trials

Randomized controlled trials may be run under ideal conditions with a narrow group of study subject characteristics to better control confounding factors and bias. These strict measures create **greater internal validity, but they decrease generalizability.**

FACTORS THAT INCREASE GENERALIZABILITY

- Broad eligibility criteria
- Multi-site studies
- Random sampling
- Observational studies

Observational studies better reflect real-world situations with increased diversity of study subjects and circumstances. There is more room for confounding factors and bias. These looser criteria result in **less internal validity and greater generalizability.**

REFERENCE
https://publications.aap.org/pediatricsinreview/article-abstract/31/8/335/33037

Topic 21: HIV Exposure in Infants – Evaluating and Managing
Evaluate and manage an infant exposed to HIV

BACKGROUND
In infants, HIV infection is life-threatening if treatment with antiretroviral therapy is not started early, so establishing a diagnosis is crucial.

EVALUATION
Testing infants for HIV is slightly more complicated than it is in older children or adults, because of the transplacental passage of maternal HIV antibodies. HIV testing in infants must be done using nucleic acid testing, not antibody-only or antigen/antibody testing. Fortunately, HIV-infected mothers who have received standard antiretroviral treatment throughout pregnancy are at low risk to transmit the infection to their infants. The infant's evaluation depends on maternal HIV status. **All infants born to HIV-positive mothers should receive post-exposure prophylaxis after birth.**

TESTING STRATEGIES
Infants born to HIV-infected mothers with low viral load (< 50 copies/ml): These infants are at low risk for vertical transmission of HIV. **Testing using an HIV nucleic acid test is done at 14-21 days after birth, again at 1-2 months of age, and again at 4-6 months of age.** Positive results are confirmed with repeat nucleic acid testing.

Infants born to HIV-infected mothers with unknown or high viral load: These infants are at increased risk of HIV infection at birth. Specific situations in which infants are considered at high risk of infection include lack of prenatal care, maternal treatment starting late in pregnancy, insufficient maternal treatment to achieve sustained viral suppression during pregnancy, or maternal detectable viral loads (> 50 copies/ml) near the time of delivery. **Testing using an HIV nucleic acid test is done at birth, then 14-21 days, then 1-2 months of age, then 2-3 months, and then 4-6 months of age.** Positive tests are confirmed with repeat nucleic acid testing.

Infants born to mothers with unknown HIV status: This would be unusual in the current era of universal maternal HIV testing. **Either the mother or the infant should have HIV antibody testing ASAP when the mother presents in labor.** These results indicate the HIV status of the mother. **If HIV testing is positive, follow the above recommendations for infants of HIV-infected mothers.**

HIV NUCLEIC ACID TESTING
HIV DNA PCR testing: This qualitative test detects proviral HIV DNA in peripheral blood mononuclear cells. This test is used frequently because test results are reliable even when infants are being treated with antiretroviral therapy. However, this test will not detect a very recent infection. Sensitivity increases after several weeks.

HIV RNA testing: A variety of methodologies are used to detect HIV RNA qualitatively or quantitatively. These tests are better at detecting infection at birth. However, if mothers or infants are being treated with effective antiretroviral treatment, there may be false negative results.

MANAGEMENT

POST-EXPOSURE PROPHYLAXIS

All infants born to HIV-infected mothers should receive prophylaxis after birth, **ideally starting within the first 6 to 12 hours of life**. The type of prophylaxis depends on maternal status. A pediatric infectious disease specialist should be involved.

Infants of at low risk of vertical transmission (viral load < 50 copies/ml): These infants require 4 weeks of zidovudine prophylaxis.

Infants at higher risk of vertical transmission: These infants require **combination prophylaxis** indefinitely with zidovudine, lamivudine, and either nevirapine or raltegravir. **This is essentially treatment** for presumed HIV.

Infants of mothers with unknown HIV status: Antibody testing of either the mother or infant should be completed ASAP. Then, **combination prophylaxis** should be started. If maternal test results are confirmed negative, the infant prophylaxis can be discontinued.

INFANTS WITH CONFIRMED POSITIVE TEST RESULTS

If repeat HIV nucleic acid testing of the infant confirms positive test results, then the combination regimen shared above should be stared or continues.

BREASTFEEDING

HIV-infected mothers should be counseled not to breastfeed. If HIV-infected mothers do choose to breastfeed their infants, the infants should undergo testing using the high-risk strategy, then every 3 months while breastfeeding, and continuing for the next 6 months after breastfeeding has ended.

REFERENCES
https://www.uptodate.com/contents/intrapartum-management-of-pregnant-women-with-hiv-and-infant-prophylaxis-in-resource-rich-settings
https://www.uptodate.com/contents/diagnostic-testing-for-hiv-infection-in-infants-and-children-younger-than-18-months

Topic 22: Hoarseness in Children – Understanding the Common Causes and Management
Understand the common causes and management of hoarseness in children

BACKGROUND
Hoarseness, or "dysphonia," can be caused by any process that affects the larynx. Most causes of pediatric hoarseness are benign and self-limited; however, some can be progressive and malignant. Some categories of hoarseness include infection, trauma, neurologic, obstruction, and congenital/structural. Here we will look at some **common causes** and treatment options.

COMMON CAUSES AND TREATMENT OPTIONS

ACUTE LARYNGITIS
Typically related to upper respiratory tract infections but can be from acute vocal strain leading to edema in the larynx (e.g., screaming at a football game or concert).
- **SYMPTOMS**: Acute infections can lead to low grade fever, hoarseness, rhinorrhea, cough, malaise.
- **TREATMENT**: This is usually self-limited. Treated conservatively with hydration, a humidifier, and vocal rest. Antibiotics and steroids are rarely needed. Steroids are only indicated if there is concern for airway compromise. Note that **whispering can actually increase the trauma** to the cords and should be avoided.

CHRONIC LARYNGITIS
Unlike acute laryngitis, chronic laryngitis is more commonly associated with environmental irritants (dry air, smoke exposure, allergens), some medications (e.g., long-term inhaled steroids), dehydration, or malignancy. Treatment depends on the etiology and includes limiting exposures to allergens, increasing hydration, humidifiers, correction of the underlying disease, and generally avoiding the environmental irritants that may be causing the chronic laryngitis.

LARYNGOTRACHEITIS "CROUP"
Very common cause of hoarseness and results in a "**barky cough**" in kids under 6 years of age. Look for the **steeple sign** on X-ray. This is **typically caused by parainfluenza.**
- **SYMPTOMS**: barky cough, low grade fever, rhinorrhea
- **TREATMENT**: Mild croup can be treated conservatively at home with humidifier, hydration, mist/steam (e.g., steaming up the bathroom), or cold air. **Steroids**, like dexamethasone or prednisone, as a single dose can shorten the duration of symptoms. For more moderate to severe croup which leads to stridor at rest, retractions, and/or respiratory distress, **nebulized epinephrine** can be administered in the ED setting along with oral or IV steroids.

VOCAL CORD NODULES
These are typically benign lesions of the vocal cords. This is a common cause of chronic hoarseness in school-aged children. Nodules can develop from overuse/trauma of the vocal cords (i.e., screaming).
- **SYMPTOMS**: A child may have a raspy voice or even difficulty breathing depending on how large the nodules are. Typically, hoarseness is **better in the morning and worse with use**.
- **TREATMENT**: Treatment is variable and ranges from watchful waiting to voice therapy to surgical correction.

GRANULOMAS

Granulomas are highly vascular growths that most often occur secondary to trauma from **intubation or prolonged intubation** but can also be a result of long-standing laryngopharyngeal reflux disease or habitual throat clearing.

- **SYMPTOMS**: hoarseness, dysphagia, cough, or feeling of a lump in the throat (globus sensation)
- **TREATMENT**: voice therapy and management of laryngopharyngeal reflux

VOCAL CORD PARALYSIS

This is commonly caused by damage to the recurrent laryngeal nerve during cardiac surgery or after **compression/injury** to the nerve after delivery (i.e., stretching the neck during a breech delivery, or compression from a cardiac malformation). Look for a baby with a high-pitched stridor, but weak cry/hoarseness since birth.

- **SYMPTOMS**: newborns tend to have weak cry and chronic aspiration (possibly even leading to recurrent pneumonias).
- **TREATMENT**: Treatment options vary from surgical intervention and reinnervation of the nerve to tracheostomy if vocal cord paralysis is bilateral and severe.

GASTROESOPHAGEAL REFLUX/LARYNGOPHARYNGEAL REFLUX

- **SYMPTOMS**: chronic cough, dysphagia, recurrent vomiting, globus sensations, bitter taste in mouth, chronic throat clearing
- **TREATMENT**: reflux medications (PPI or H2 blocker), diet modifications

LARYNGOMALACIA

There is a collapse of the supraglottic airway during inspiration. This is the most common congenital anomaly leading to stridor in infants.

- **SYMPTOMS**: The main symptom is **monophasic, inspiratory stridor** during the neonatal period (as opposed to tracheomalacia causing biphasic stridor from malformations like vascular rings). The typical onset of stridor occurs around 4-6 weeks of age, it gets louder around 4-8 months of age, and resolves by 12-18 months. Classically, this **stridor gets worse in the supine position and improves when prone**.
- **TREATMENT**: Watchful waiting when laryngomalacia is mild and causing no significant symptoms is appropriate.

TUMORS

Papillomatosis is a benign tumor most often diagnosed between the ages 2-3 years of age. It is thought to be caused by the HPV virus (commonly HPV6 and HPV11) and acquired during passage through the birth canal of an infected mother. Treatment typically involves surgical resection.

REFERENCES
https://www.uptodate.com/contents/common-causes-of-hoarseness-in-children
https://publications.aap.org/pediatricsinreview/article-abstract/27/6/e47/34145

Topic 23: Hypoglycemia in Children – Evaluating and Managing
Evaluate and manage a child with hypoglycemia

BACKGROUND

Disorders causing hypoglycemia are rare but dangerous. Exposure to prolonged hypoglycemic episodes can cause **seizures and brain damage**. Multiple body systems work to maintain glucose levels within a normal range. When one or more of these systems fail, blood sugars drop, and the brain does not have enough of its preferred fuel, glucose. **Evaluation and safe management of patients in whom hypoglycemia is suspected is very important to prevent developmental delays and disabilities.**

In response to fasting, several metabolic and hormonal changes should occur. First, insulin is suppressed and the counterregulatory hormones (growth hormone, cortisol, glucagon, and epinephrine) rise. The liver then becomes the main source of glucose. In the liver, glycogen is broken down to produce glucose (glycogenolysis) and glucose is produced from amino acids, glycerol, and lactate (gluconeogenesis). With longer fasting times, adipose tissue then becomes the source of fuel. Fatty tissue is broken down to produce free fatty acids (lipolysis) and ketones such as beta-hydroxybutyrate (ketogenesis). Out of necessity, the brain then switches from its preferred source of fuel (glucose) to ketones.

Hypoglycemia occurs when one or more of these normal responses to fasting does not function as expected. These disorders can be divided into four categories:
- Disorders of excess insulin
- Ketotic hypoglycemia
- Fatty acid oxidation disorders
- Disorders of gluconeogenesis

EVALUATION

An evaluation looking for the cause of hypoglycemia is recommended in patients after the first 48 hours of life. Until then, neonates are transitioning to extrauterine life, their plasma glucose levels may be lower. If there are persistent glucose levels **<60 mg/dl measured in a lab** (point-of-care testing is insufficient evidence), then proceed further with evaluations.

Once hypoglycemia has been documented, the next step is a systematic evaluation to determine the cause. Important details and diagnostic clues can be obtained from the history and physical. **Laboratory evaluation includes a "critical sample" obtained when the plasma glucose is < 50 mg/dl**. This critical sample should **include tests of the hormones and metabolic fuels** (more on this later in this topic summary).

HISTORY

The age at presentation can help to narrow the differential diagnosis. Neonates and infants are more likely to have hyperinsulinism, panhypopituitarism, inborn errors of metabolism, or disorders of gluconeogenesis. **Toddlers** are more likely to have glycogen storage disorders, ingestions, idiopathic ketotic hypoglycemia, or growth hormone or cortisol deficiencies. **In older children and adolescents**, it is important to consider factitious hypoglycemia, toxic ingestions, and insulinoma in the differential.

Investigate the frequency of hypoglycemic episode when fasting. Episodes occurring after only a few hours of fasting are more likely due to hyperinsulinism or one of the more severe glycogen storage disorders (type I or III). The list of potential causes is broader with longer fasting duration before hypoglycemia.

Investigate foods triggers that may be causing hypoglycemic episodes. The caregiver may be able to describe a pattern of symptoms after consumption of fructose (raising concern for **hereditary fructose intolerance**) or milk products (raising concern for **galactosemia**).

Investigate the possibility of toxic ingestions. Ask about medications in the home with a specific focus on diabetes medications (e.g., sulfonylureas) or beta-blockers, and ask about the possibility of ethanol ingestion.

PHYSICAL EXAM

Height and weight should be measured and plotted. These findings, in conjunction with hypoglycemia, may narrow your differential:

- **SHORT STATURE AND A SLOW GROWTH VELOCITY**: Consider growth hormone deficiency.
- **HEPATOMEGALY**: Consider glycogen storage disorders.
- **POOR WEIGHT GAIN**: Consider adrenal insufficiency, glycogen storage disease, and idiopathic ketotic hypoglycemia.
- **MIDLINE DEFECTS, A MICROPENIS, OR UNDESCENDED TESTICLES**: Consider hypopituitarism.
- **TALL STATURE, MACROGLOSSIA, ABDOMINAL WALL DEFECTS**: Consider Beckwith-Wiedeman syndrome.
- **HYPERPIGMENTATION**: This may indicate primary adrenal insufficiency.

LABORATORY EVALUATION

The bedrock of the laboratory evaluation of hypoglycemia is the **"critical sample"** obtained at a time of hypoglycemia (serum glucose < 50 mg/dl). The critical sample includes tests of hormones and fuels, and should include:

- Serum glucose
- Insulin
- C-peptide
- Beta-hydroxybutyrate
- CMP
- Free fatty acids
- Lactate
- Ammonia
- Cortisol
- Growth hormone
- Acyl-carnitine profile
- Free and total carnitines
- Urine for ketones if beta-hydroxybutyrate testing is not available.

If symptoms are suggestive of hypoglycemia, immediately check blood sugar using a **point-of-care device before giving any treatment**. If this patient is not on insulin, or does not have a known cause of hypoglycemia, make every effort to **obtain the "critical" blood sample before giving treatment**. If possible, collect the **first urine sample after the episode** and send it to the lab.

If the history suggests the **possibility of toxic ingestions**, those substances should be tested for specifically. The results of the critical sample will indicate in which of the **four categories** the pathology lies. Further specific testing, including **genetic testing**, may be necessary.

MANAGEMENT

If the point-of-care test result shows a blood sugar < 70 mg/dl, and if the patient is symptomatic, give 10 – 20 grams of **fast-acting carbohydrates ASAP** (corn syrup, crackers, juice, sugar, soda) orally if the patient is awake and **able to eat/drink and swallow safely**. Some possible options, and portions, are listed below:

- Glucose tablets (4 or 5 grams per tablet)
- Glucose gel (15 grams per tube)
- Juice (12 grams per 4 oz)
- Soda (not diet soda) (18 gram per 6 oz)
- Honey (17 gram per 1 tablespoon)
- Table sugar (12.5 gram per 1 tablespoon)
- Fruit (approximately 15 grams per four ounces)

If there is altered mental status:

- Glucagon 0.5 mg (patient < 25 kg) or 1.0 mg (patient >25 kg) IM or SC
- IV bolus of D10 2 ml/kg infused over a few minutes

Check blood sugar every 10 - 15 minutes until > 70 mg/dl, then every 30 – 60 minutes until stable. If the blood sugar level is low, repeat the carbohydrate bolus. If repeated carbohydrate boluses are needed, an IV infusion of dextrose will be needed.

If the situation is more emergent, give a dextrose bolus via IV and consider a drip. For infants and young children, give 2 ml/kg of D10 (the max dose is 500 ml, which equals 50 grams of dextrose). For adolescents, simply give ½ –1 ampule of D50 (contains 12.5 - 25 grams of dextrose). After the initial treatment, establish IV access (if not done already) and start IV fluids containing D10. Titrate infusion rate to maintain plasma glucose in a safe range (typically 70 – 120 mg/dl).

PEARL: Percent solutions refer to grams/100 ml. For example, D50 refers to 50 grams of dextrose per 100 ml water. So, a 50 ml "ampule" of D50 contains 25 grams of dextrose.

Glucagon may also be used to increase glucose levels when the cause of the hypoglycemia is excess insulin (endogenous or exogenous). In order for glucagon to work, there must be adequate glycogen stores and adrenal insufficiency should not be present.

REFERENCES
https://www.uptodate.com/contents/approach-to-hypoglycemia-in-infants-and-children
https://www.jpeds.com/article/S0022-3476(15)00358-3/fulltext

Topic 24: Hypospadias in a Neonate – Recognizing and Managing
Recognize and manage hypospadias in a neonate

BACKGROUND
Hypospadias is a condition in males in which the urethra is located on the underside of the penis rather than the tip of the penis. This condition occurs in about 1 in 300 male births. There is a **strong genetic component** with a 14% recurrence rate among male siblings and 8% recurrence rate in male offspring. It can be associated with other genetic syndromes (including Denys-Drash syndrome, WAGR syndrome, and Opitz syndrome). As such, **when you see a hypospadias, do a complete physical exam to look for other congenital anomalies which might connect the hypospadias to a broader syndrome.**

Other possible etiologies include environmental exposures, possible "endocrine disrupters" involved (e.g., maternal exposure to DES), and early exposure to progesterone (e.g., a mothers given progesterone for a threatened abortion).

RECOGNIZING HYPOSPADIAS
Hypospadias is generally an abnormal **ventral and more proximal** placement of the urethral opening. When discussing this topic, note that proximal refers to the base of the penis and distal refers to anything closer to the head of the penis. The following image will help you familiarize yourself with the dorsal and proximal orientation of penile anatomy.
IMAGE: www.pbrlinks.com/2023MOCA-PENILE-ANATOMY

PHYSICAL EXAM
The genital exam should include:
- Measurement of stretched penile length
- Assessment of penile curvature
- Assessment of the foreskin
- Confirmation of the presence of both testicles in the normal scrotal position

CLASSIFICATIONS
- **STANDARD HYPOSPADIAS**: There is a misplaced urethral opening. Penis size is normal, and the curvature is typically within normal. The type of hypospadias can be subdivided by its placement on the penile shaft.
    - **Distal**: The ectopic (misplaced) urethra is at the coronal edge, or more distal.
    - **Proximal**: The ectopic urethra is midshaft, or lower towards the scrotum.
- **SEVERE HYPOSPADIAS**: The urethral opening is **in the scrotum**. There may be an associated **micropenis** (< 2.5cm stretched length in full term infants), and there will **likely be the presence of severe chordee** (congenital penile curvature in which the penis bends or twists when erect).
    - Boys with severe hypospadias are likely to have **other non-genital anomalies**.
    - These are also seen often with cryptorchidism.
- **FORME FRUSTE**: There appear to be two urethras at the tip of the glans, however one is a blind pit. There may be asymmetry of the foreskin, making circumcision difficult.
    - **IMAGE**: www.pbrlinks.com/2023MOCA-FORME-FRUSTE

OTHER VARIANTS & ASSOCIATIONS

- **MEGAMEATUS**: Results as one, very large urethral opening. It is sometimes described as a "catfish" mouth. This is typically noted at the time of circumcision (complete circumcision may proceed as usual).
    - **IMAGE**: www.pbrlinks.com/2023MOCA-MEGAMEATUS
- **CHORDEE WITH NORMAL MEATUS**: As mentioned above, "chordee" refers to a congenital penile curvature in which the penis bends or twists when erect. This may visually appear as though the ventral foreskin is "tethering" the tip downwards. The foreskin overlying the urethra will typically be very thin.
    - **IMAGE**: www.pbrlinks.com/2023MOCA-CHORDEE
- **CRYPTORCHIDISM**: If there is the combination of cryptorchidism (in which at least testicle is undescended) with hypospadias, there is a high probability of a Disorder of Sex Development (DSD, or ambiguous genitalia).
- **INCOMPLETE FORESKIN**: The ventral part of the foreskin is "missing," creating what's called a "dorsal hooded." The foreskin in these patients does not fully retract.
    - **IMAGE**: www.pbrlinks.com/2023MOCA-INCOMPLETE

MANAGEMENT

The management **depends on the severity** of the hypospadias. Generally, the more proximal the urethral placement, the more severe it is. Renal imaging is not recommended for isolated hypospadias unless the patient is febrile or has a symptomatic urinary tract infection.

IMAGE: www.pbrlinks.com/2023MOCA-SEVERITY (Increasing Severity)

- **STANDARD HYPOSPADIAS**: Delay circumcision and refer to urology. Urology will perform a repair of the hypospadias simultaneously with complete circumcision (if desired by the parents).
- **SEVERE HYPOSPADIAS**: Obtain a karyotype to confirm the presence of a Y chromosome and consider serum electrolytes to screen for congenital adrenal hyperplasia (CAH). Refer to a urologist and consider getting Genetics and Endocrinology consultations.
- **FORME FRUSTE**: If this is found after starting a circumcision, then complete the circumcision. If circumcision has not been performed, but is desired, **delay the circumcision** until it can be done in the operating room. For simple forme fruste, there is no need for urological referral.
- **MEGAMEATUS**: Refer to Urology for possible urethroplasty in the future. If megameatus is found after starting a circumcision, then complete the circumcision. If circumcision has not been performed, but is desired, **delay the circumcision** until the Urology referral.
- **CHORDEE WITH NORMAL URETHRAL MEATUS**: Delay circumcision until approximately 6-12 months of age and refer to urology. These children may have difficulties with erections later in life.
- **CRYPTORCHIDISM**: Obtain a karyotype to confirm the presence of a Y chromosome and consider serum electrolytes to screen for congenital adrenal hyperplasia (CAH).
- **MICROPENIS**: When there is the combination of hypospadias and micropenis, hormone therapy (i.e., testosterone therapy once per month for 3 months) can be considered.

REFERENCES

https://www.uptodate.com/contents/hypospadias-pathogenesis-diagnosis-and-evaluation

Topic 25: Introducing Solid Foods (Including Highly Allergenic Foods) to Infants – Understanding Current Recommendations

Understand current recommendations for introducing solid foods (including highly allergenic foods) to infants

BACKGROUND

Guidelines universally recommend that **solids should be introduced by approximately 6 months of age in all infants while allowing breastmilk to constitute most of the infant's nutrition though the first 6 months of life**. The following sections summarize recommendations for introducing solids and highly allergenic foods to infants.

INTRODUCTION OF SOLIDS

Early introduction of solids before 4 months is associated with increased weight gain in infancy and childhood. **Delayed introduction beyond 6 months** is associated with iron deficiency anemia.

For most infants, **solids (purees to start) and a sippy cup (training cup) should be introduced at approximately 4-6 months of age. Healthy snacks should be introduced at approximately 9 months** of age at a frequency of twice per day. Solids should be introduced **1 new ingredient every 3-5 days to allow identification of food-related reactions**. Fruit and vegetable purees should be encouraged, but **no juice**. Early foods being introduced should include iron and zinc-containing foods.

Milestones for readiness include:

- Holds head independently when sitting in a highchair
- Opens mouth to food
- Shows interest in others eating
- Weighs at least twice the birth weight

INTRODUCTION OF HIGHLY ALLERGENIC FOODS

The most common highly allergenic foods among infants and toddlers include **cows' milk, eggs, soy, and wheat,** whereas in children they include **peanuts, seafood, sesame, and tree nuts.** There is growing understanding of a **critical window where risk modification is possible** for infants at elevated risk of developing food allergies. While prior AAP 2000 guidelines had recommended delayed introduction of highly allergenic foods beyond 1 year, since 2008 **AAP guidelines recommend introduction of highly allergenic foods between 4-6 months** at home (with oral antihistamines available if the child has signs of atopy or strong family history). If food allergy testing has been done, **do not restrict foods based solely on IgE results**. Food allergies are clinical diagnoses. Generally, you must have a historical reaction to support the diagnosis of a food allergy.

PEANUT INTRODUCTION

Special risk-stratified guidance is available regarding the introduction of peanuts based on their history of eczema.

- **NO ECZEMA OR FOOD ALLERGIES**: Introduction peanuts to the child at 6 months of age at home.
- **MILD-MODERATE ECZEMA**: Introduction of peanuts to the child at 6 months of age at home.
- **SEVERE ECZEMA OR EGG ALLERGY**: Allergy testing should be done by IgE or skin prick test before introducing peanuts.
  - **IF TESTING IS NEGATIVE**: May introduce peanuts at home OR in a supervised office setting at 4-6 months of age based on preference. If child does well, continue to provide peanuts at least 3 times per week.
  - **IF TESTING POSITIVE**: Refer to a specialist. Based on the degree of positivity, either a graded oral food challenge will be done, or the recommendation will be to avoid peanuts and treat the child as allergic. If deemed allergic, note that peanuts are legumes but 25%-50% of patients are also allergic to tree nuts. Also, guidance should be provided around the issue of cross contamination in factories processing peanuts and true tree nuts.

REFERENCES

https://www.uptodate.com/contents/introducing-highly-allergenic-foods-to-infants-and-children
https://publications.aap.org/pediatricsinreview/article/40/5/211/35279/Infant-Peanut-Introduction-Simplified
https://www.aap.org/en/patient-care/healthy-active-living-for-families/infant-food-and-feeding/
https://healthychildren.org/English/ages-stages/baby/feeding-nutrition/Pages/Starting-Solid-Foods.aspx

Topic 26: Microcephaly in Infants – Evaluating
Evaluate an infant with microcephaly

BACKGROUND
Microcephaly can be caused by genetic or environmental factors. Any child with microcephaly should be evaluated to understand the cause of the microcephaly in order to address avoidable complications.

EVALUATION
Microcephaly is defined as the occipitofrontal circumference (OFC) > 2 SD below the mean, which usually means < 3rd percentile. Evaluation should be initiated when a single measurement is more than 2 SD below the mean, or when there is a progressive decrease in head size over time (i.e., crossing two major percentiles). **Prenatal microcephaly** is found on ultrasound evaluation and is defined as a head circumference that is < 3 SD below the mean or below the 2nd percentile for gestational age. A **normal newborn head circumference** (HC) is approximately 35 cm. After that, it increases by approximately 1 cm/month for 6 months and then ½ cm/month from 6 – 12 months.

Elements of the evaluation process are discussed below. However, UpToDate offers and excellent algorithm which is being made for your review:
- **IMAGE**: www.pbrlinks.com/2023MOCA-microcephaly

HISTORY
Microcephaly may be present at birth, or it may develop after birth.

Primary microcephaly occurs when the head circumference is **abnormal at birth**. A **detailed family medical history and prenatal history should be taken, including** the history of any genetic defects in the family, maternal exposure to medications, maternal drug use, maternal alcohol use, maternal infections while pregnant, parental consanguinity, and maternal health problems.

Acquired microcephaly occurs when the head circumference is **normal at birth and then falls off the curve** over months to years. A detailed history should be taken including the same history discussed above. **Additional history** should include head circumference (HC) at birth, the HC trajectory, the patient's developmental history, illnesses since birth, medications being taken,

ETIOLOGIES
Potential causes of microcephaly include:
- **Autosomal dominant disorders**
- **Autosomal recessive disorders**
- **Trisomy 13, 18, and 21**
- **Cornelia de Lange syndrome** (upturned nose, eyebrows that meet in the middle, cleft palate, GERD)
- **Smith-Lemli-Opitz syndrome** (defective cholesterol synthesis and possible 2-3 toe syndactyly)
- **Rett syndrome** (regression of milestones)
- **Inborn errors of metabolism** (variable presentations, but likely with issues early in life)
- **Hypothyroidism** (decreased activity, constipation, weight gain, slow growth)

- **TORCH infections** include Toxoplasma, Other (Varicella, Syphilis), Rubella, Cytomegalovirus (CMV), and Herpes Simplex Virus (HSV). Look for neurological deficits, calcifications on neuroimaging, eye abnormalities, blueberry muffin syndrome.
- **Maternal phenylketonuria** (PKU) (eczematous rash)
- **Fanconi anemia** (short stature, café au lait spots, renal abnormalities, hypogonadism, and upper limb/hand anomalies, aplastic anemia with macrocytosis)
- **Cri-Du-Chat syndrome** (high-pitched cry, developmental delay, wide-set eyes, high palate, possible VSD)
- **Familial microcephaly**

PHYSICAL EXAM

Do a thorough physical exam to look for clues about the etiology, including syndromic features and:
- Evaluate shape of head
- Assessing fontanelle patency
- Assess milestones
- Skin exam
- Ophthalmologic exam
- Neurologic exam
- Assess for abnormalities of the digits and extremities
- Weight and length trajectories
- Organomegaly

PARENTAL OFC

Parents head circumferences should be obtained and plotted on *The Weaver Curve* to assess familial variation. **Familial microcephaly can be followed clinically**, and additional evaluation would be initiated if there are any developmental or neurological concerns.

DIAGNOSTIC TESTING

Testing is dictated by the differential diagnosis created at the time of the history and physical exam.

GENETIC TESTING

If the child has dysmorphic features or abnormal development, this may warrant genetic testing (i.e., genomic array). However, this is **usually done in conjunction with referral to a specialist**.

NEUROIMAGING

Neuroimaging studies may identify structural causes for microcephaly. MRI is the preferred imaging modality. However, if you are concerned about TORCH infection or craniosynostosis then CT may be better to identify bony structures and microcalcifications.

OTHER TESTING & EVALUATIONS

A multidisciplinary approach may be needed to complete the evaluation process. If concerns exist for possible congenital infections, consult an infectious diseases specialist. If eye abnormalities exist, refer to an ophthalmologist for guidance on additional possible diagnoses.

REFERENCES

https://www.uptodate.com/contents/microcephaly-in-infants-and-children-etiology-and-evaluation
https://publications.aap.org/pediatricsinreview/article/31/9/382/33027/Abnormal-Head-Growth

Topic 27: Microscopic Hematuria in Children – Evaluating
Evaluate a child with microscopic hematuria

BACKGROUND
The **gold standard** for detecting **microscopic hematuria** is examination of a sample under 40x magnification using a **microscope**. It is diagnosed when there are **at least 5 RBCs per high-powered field**. In children, microscopic hematuria is a **common incidental finding** and **usually benign**.

ETIOLOGIES OF PERSISTENT HEMATURIA
Persistent hematuria is defined as having a **positive repeat test six months apart**. The most common causes of persistent hematuria in children are **glomerulopathies, hypercalciuria, and nutcracker syndrome**.

IGA NEPHROPATHY
IgA nephropathy can present as persistent microscopic hematuria with **episodes of gross hematuria**, usually after a **URI or GI related illness**. A **renal biopsy** can be used for diagnosis, which would show **mesangial IgA deposits** under an immunofluorescence study.

ALPORT SYNDROME
Alport syndrome is a **recessive X-linked disorder**, therefore it usually seen in **males**. It is associated with hereditary nephritis and hematuria. Affected male patients can present with **sensorineural hearing loss**, **anterior lenticonus** of their eyes, and **progressive renal failure**. Affected **females who are heterozygous carriers can have hematuria**, but usually do not progress to renal failure. Diagnosis is made with a **renal biopsy** showing a thin glomerular basement membrane. **Genetic testing** may also identify mutations in collagen genes.

THIN BASEMENT MEMBRANE DISEASE (AKA BENIGN FAMILIAL HEMATURIA)
This is an **autosomal dominant** disorder. Patients will usually have a **family history significant for hematuria without progressive renal disease**. A **renal biopsy** can be used for diagnosis, which would show a thin glomerular basement membrane under electron microscopy.

POSTSTREPTOCOCCAL GLOMERULONEPHRITIS
This can have a **range** of presentations, usually after a **skin or throat** infection from **group A strep (GAS)**. Although an acute nephritic syndrome can occur, the most common presentation is **asymptomatic microscopic hematuria** which usually **resolves after 3-6 months**. Look for evidence of a recent strep infection (ASO titers).

HYPERCALCIURIA
For children who are at least 6 years old, a **urine calcium to creatinine ratio greater than 0.2** is diagnostic of hypercalciuria which can also be associated with **asymptomatic microscopic hematuria**.

NEPHROLITHIASIS AND NEPHROCALCINOSIS
Patients are **more likely to present with gross hematuria and abdominal pain**, but they can present with **microscopic hematuria without abdominal pain**.

NUTCRACKER SYNDROME

When the **left renal vein is compressed between the proximal superior mesenteric artery and the aorta**, it can result in hematuria in children and is called Nutcracker Syndrome. It is diagnosed with either a **Doppler US or CT scan**. Although patients are **usually asymptomatic, left flank pain** can sometimes be present.

ETIOLOGIES OF TRANSIENT HEMATURIA

UTIs, fever, exercise, and trauma are the most common causes of **transient hematuria** in children. If diagnosed, repeat a urinalysis 2 weeks later. If still present and decreasing, may repeat again 2 weeks after that.

DIAGNOSTIC EVALUATIONS

Depending on the clinical presentation of the patient, the diagnostic evaluations can differ.

ISOLATED ASYMPTOMATIC MICROSCOPIC HEMATURIA

The most common presentation of **microscopic hematuria is isolated, asymptomatic, and transient**. As a result, simply **observing** the patient and **repeating the urinalysis** is the initial approach. The patient's **blood pressure and urinalysis** should be repeated **weekly for two weeks**. Since exercise can induce hematuria, the physician should ensure the patient was **not exercising prior** to repeat urine samples.

If the patient becomes **symptomatic** (hypertension, gross hematuria, proteinuria, etc.) at any time during this initial two-week observation time, then the physician should conduct a **thorough evaluation**.

If the patient **remains asymptomatic but has persistent hematuria**, then the physician should obtain a **urine culture**. **If the urine culture is positive**, then the appropriate antibiotics should be given for treatment. **If the urine culture is negative**, then the patient should continue to be observed with repeated blood pressure measurements and urinalyses every 3-6 months.

If the isolated asymptomatic microscopic hematuria persists for one year, then the physician should conduct the following evaluations to search for **potential causes**: check for **hypercalciuria** by measuring the urine calcium to creatinine ratio, check for the possibility of **genetic causes** such as **Alport Syndrome** or **thin basement membrane disease** by testing first degree relatives for microscopic hematuria, check for the possibility of **sickle cell trait** by performing a hemoglobin analysis, and checking for **Nutcracker Syndrome** with a Doppler US.

ASYMPTOMATIC MICROSCOPIC HEMATURIA WITH PROTEINURIA

Since the **combination of hematuria with proteinuria places the patient at a higher risk** of significant renal disease, patients with this presentation **should be evaluated further by** measuring their serum creatinine and quantifying their proteinuria with either a 24-hour urine collection or a first morning urine sample to test for the urine protein to creatine ratio.

If the **protein excretion in the 24-hour urine collection sample is greater than 4mg/m^2 per hour** or the first morning urine sample has a **urine protein to creatinine ratio greater than 0.2**, then the physician should **refer the patient to a pediatric nephrologist** since there is a high likelihood that the child has significant renal disease.

If the protein excretion is less than the above values, then the physician should repeat labs again in 2-3 weeks. If both hematuria and proteinuria resolved, there is no need for further evaluation. If the proteinuria resolved and only the hematuria remains, then the patient should get the workup outlined above for isolated asymptomatic microscopic hematuria. If the proteinuria remains, then the physician should refer the patient to a pediatric nephrologist for further evaluation.

SYMPTOMATIC MICROSCOPIC HEMATURIA

Obtaining a further history and performing a thorough physical exam can help to identify a specific cause for symptomatic microscopic hematuria. Physicians should ask about a history of any recent trauma, symptoms suggestive of a UTI (incontinence, dysuria, urgency, or frequency), unilateral flank pain and whether it radiates to the groin or not (kidney stone vs pyelonephritis), pharyngitis or impetigo, URI symptoms, history of sickle cell disease or trait, history of hemophilia, deafness, family history of hematuria or renal disease, family history of kidney stones, and a review of the patient's medications for potential causes of interstitial nephritis. Physicians should also look for symptoms on physical exam such as abnormal blood pressure readings, edema, weight gain, purpura, and abdominal discomfort or masses like in Wilms tumor.

REFERENCES

https://www.uptodate.com/contents/evaluation-of-microscopic-hematuria-in-children

Topic 28: Myocarditis – Recognizing the Clinical Manifestations, Etiology, and Diagnosis

Recognize the clinical manifestations, etiology, and diagnosis of myocarditis

BACKGROUND

Myocarditis in children is a disease that causes inflammation of the heart's myocardium. It may be due to infection, exposure to toxins, or due to autoimmune diseases.

ETIOLOGIES

INFECTIONS

Infectious causes of myocarditis in children are the most common. Viral myocarditis can be due to coxsackie group B (an enterovirus), adenovirus, EBV, CMV, parvovirus B19, or HHV type 6. The SARS-CoV-2 virus can mimic symptoms of an acute viral myocarditis in children with multisystem inflammatory syndrome in children (MIS-C).

DRUG HYPERSENSITIVITY

Certain medications can cause drug hypersensitivity in children, which can lead to myocarditis. The most common drugs include antibiotics (azithromycin, beta-lactams, tetracycline, and minocycline), CNS drugs (benzodiazepines, carbamazepine, phenytoin, clozapine, and TCAs), vaccines (mRNA SARS-CoV-2 vaccine), anti-tuberculosis drugs, and diuretics (furosemide, hydrochlorothiazide).

AUTOIMMUNE DISEASES

Autoimmune diseases can present with myocarditis as a cardiac complication in children. The most common autoimmune diseases associated with myocarditis include systemic lupus erythematosus (SLE), granulomatosis with polyangiitis, Takayasu arteritis, and giant cell arteritis.

CLINICAL MANIFESTATIONS

CLINICAL PRESENTATION

Myocarditis can present with a variety of symptoms. Since the most common cause of pediatric myocarditis is from an infection, **it is common for patients to have a history of a recent viral respiratory or GI illness with symptoms such as fever, myalgias, malaise, abdominal pain, or vomiting within the past 2 weeks.** At initial presentation, **children may have signs of heart** failure, such as dyspnea at rest, tachycardia, tachypnea, exercise intolerance, syncope, or hepatomegaly. **Supraventricular arrhythmias, ventricular arrhythmias, or a complete heart block** may also occur which can potentially lead to a sudden and unexpected death. A patient **may also become hemodynamically compromised** with a decreased cardiac output that can present as hypotension, poor perfusion, weak pulses, acidosis, or hepatomegaly. Fulminant myocarditis can lead to cardiogenic shock and death.

PHYSICAL EXAM FINDINGS

Although certain symptoms can be seen in patients, **there are no specific physical exam findings for diagnosing myocarditis.** Examples of possible symptoms include an S3 or S4 heart sound, heart murmurs indicating an insufficiency in the function of either the mitral or tricuspid valve, hypotension, poor perfusion, weak pulses, edema, hepatomegaly, tachypnea, retractions, rales, and altered mental status.

DIAGNOSIS

ENDOMYOCARDIAL BIOPSY (EMB)

Although the sensitivity is low, and the risks of the procedure are high since the patient will need to be intubated, **the gold standard for diagnosing myocarditis in children is an endomyocardial biopsy**. The specimen is then viewed under light microscopy and the Dallas Criteria is used to see if the sample meets the criteria of myocarditis.

CARDIAC MAGNETIC RESONANCE (CMR)

Cardiac magnetic resonance is starting to become more popular for diagnosing myocarditis in children because it is non-invasive. CMR images can help detect the location and extent of the myocardial inflammation in the patient. Although CMR is non-invasive, younger patients may need to be sedated and intubated for the procedure, which then carries similar risks of adverse events to endomyocardial biopsy.

CLINICAL DIAGNOSIS

If EMB or CMR are unavailable or deemed too risky, myocarditis can also be diagnosed clinically if some of the following are present and the clinical scenario seems to fit this diagnosis:

- Elevated troponin
- EKG showing ventricular dysfunction
- EKG suggestive of an arrhythmia or an acute myocardial injury
- Physical symptoms of cardiac dysfunction (e.g., dyspnea, tachycardia, a gallop, tachypnea, exertional chest pain, exercise intolerance, syncope, or hepatomegaly)
- A prodromal respiratory or GI illness that occurred within the past 2 weeks

REFERENCES

https://www.uptodate.com/contents/clinical-manifestations-and-diagnosis-of-myocarditis-in-children
https://www.uptodate.com/contents/myocarditis-causes-and-pathogenesis

Topic 29: Oral Health Risks – Screening and Managing Appropriately
Screen for oral health risks and manage appropriately

BACKGROUND
Many of the oral health diseases in children, including dental caries, start at an early age. Therefore, it is important to screen and counsel children and parents to ensure they are receiving routine dental care to prevent oral health problems.

SCREENING
Most children's first teeth erupt around 5-8 months of age. **The AAP recommends children get an oral health assessment by 6 months old and have their first dental visit at or near 12 months old.** The physician should continue doing oral health assessments in children at the 12, 18, 24, and 30-month well-child visits and at 3, 4, 5, and 6-year well-child visits if the child has not already established care with a dentist. A dental referral should be given to children around 1 year old.

During the screenings, physicians should look for the following on physical exam:
- Abnormalities of either the teeth or oral mucosa
- Signs of dental plaque
- White spots on teeth
- Cavities

While wearing gloves, the physician should use a light and disposable mouth mirror to inspect the teeth. Then, a soft-bristled toothbrush should be used to gently remove any visible plaque an then the teeth should be reexamined.

RISK ASSESSMENT
A dental risk assessment should be done prior to 3 years of age to identify risk factors that can be addressed to help prevent future oral health issues. **An early dental referral for preventative care should be given to children with the following oral health risk factors:**
- Caregiver with active caries
- Low socioeconomic status
- Exposure to tobacco smoke at home
- Special needs child
- Breast or bottle feeding after 1 year of age
- Frequently eating or drinking of sugary foods and beverages
- Prolonged use of a sippy cup
- Using a bottle at bedtime
- Taking liquid medications for over 3 weeks
- Inadequate exposure to fluoride.
- Exam showing plaque on the child's upper front teeth
- Exam showing enamel defects, such as pits or stains

NONNUTRITIVE SUCKING

Counsel families on nonnutritive sucking **before the child's primary teeth erupt**. Nonnutritive sucking includes sucking on things like a pacifier or thumb to self-soothe. Nonnutritive sucking **should be discontinued by 24 months of age** since it may lead to the child developing malocclusion.

TEETHING

Counsel parents on teething **before the child's primary teeth erupt**. Children who are teething may be irritable, excessively drool, and seek to chew on objects. **Teething should be managed with symptomatic care** (e.g., chilled teething ring, chew toys, or acetaminophen).

DIETARY HABITS

BREAST MILK AND FORMULA

Parents should be counseled on their child's dietary habits as their primary teeth erupt. Once the patient is **6 months old, solid food can be introduced**. Breast or formula feeding should continue until 12 months old. **A sippy cup (training cup) can be used at around 6 months old** to help decrease the duration of exposure of breastmilk or formula on the patient's primary teeth. **A bottle should not be used after 12 months old.**

JUICE AND SUGARY DRINKS

Juice and sugary drinks have a high risk for causing dental caries. 100% fruit juice should not be given to children younger than 12 months of age and should be limited to only 4 oz per day for children who are 1-3 years old. Other sugary drinks, like flavored milk, soda, and other fruit juices, should not be given to children younger than 5 years old. Parents should be counseled to encourage their child to drink from an open cup rather than a sippy cup, rinse the mouth with water after consuming anything sugary, and avoid sugary drinks throughout childhood.

ORAL HYGIENE

Counsel parents **cleaning teeth twice daily for two minutes using a toothpaste that contains fluoride.** Parents can **begin flossing once** the space in between their child's teeth becomes too small for only the toothbrush to clean. Children should have their toothbrushing and flossing **supervised by their parents until they are at least 8 years old**.

FLUORIDE

Counsel parents on fluoride supplementation prior to the 6-month well-child visit. The AAP recommends that **all children with teeth at any age should be using fluoride-containing toothpaste** to brush their teeth. Although the use of fluoride is the most important way to prevent dental caries, **too much fluoride supplementation can cause dental fluorosis** (white streaks in the permanent teeth enamel). Therefore, parents should be instructed on how much fluoride-containing toothpaste to use for their child with these general recommendations about the amount of toothpaste to use:

- CHILDREN YOUNGER THAN 3 YEARS OF AGE: grain of rice
- 3 YEARS OF AGE: size of a pea
- OLDER THAN 3 YEARS OF AGE: Slightly larger than a pea

Fluoride supplementation and topical fluoride application should not be given to all patients. It should only be considered in patients who are at high risk of dental caries since the combination of fluoridated toothpaste and fluoridated drinking water (which most states have) provides enough protection against dental caries for low-risk patients.

REFERENCES

https://www.uptodate.com/contents/preventive-dental-care-and-counseling-for-infants-and-young-children

Topic 30: Parental Refusal of Immunizations or Other Treatments – Recognizing and Applying Ethical Principles

Recognize and apply ethical principles regarding parental refusal of immunizations or other treatments

BACKGROUND

Vaccine hesitancy is defined as refusing or delaying the acceptance of vaccination despite vaccines being available. Although every state in the US requires certain vaccines for school entry, **parents can refuse vaccines for any of the three exempt reasons:**

- Medical
- Religious
- Philosophical.

About one-third to one-half of vaccine hesitant parents will eventually agree to vaccinate their children, therefore it is important to approach these parents in a structured and ethical manner.

APPROACH TO PARENTS

ESTABLISH A POSITIVE DIALOGUE

From the initial visit and continuing with all subsequent visits, **physicians should make sure to listen respectfully and use positive, nonconfrontational, and nonjudgmental language**. This will help to establish and maintain trust for each visit. Physicians should also take time to share the following with parents:

- The shared goal of doing what is best for the child
- The vast amount of complex and sometimes conflicting information about the benefits and safety of vaccines
- An offer to help collect and interpret information from the best sources for the parents to make a more informed decision

IDENTIFY PARENTAL CONCERNS

Physicians should be careful not to make any assumptions about why the parent is refusing vaccines. **Parental concerns can be affected or influenced by misinformation from outside factors** such as other family members or friends, their religious community, the news, internet, or social media. Personal parental concerns can stem from fear of medical interventions, conspiracy theories, or nonconformity.

TARGET EDUCATION

Most parents are open to discussion with their pediatrician. **Physicians should be careful not to use difficult medical or scientific vocabulary that may confuse parents.** Pictures may also be helpful in explaining topics to parents. **The following topics are some examples that can be used to educate parents about vaccines:**

- Benefits and limitations
- Safety and adverse side-effects
- Natural infection risks
- Reviewing and correcting misinformation
- Pain with injections

In order to establish trust and credibility, physicians should be honest and let parents know that although vaccines have benefits, **the limitations are that they are not 100% effective, and they are not 100% risk free**. Vaccines are licensed by the FDA after being fully tested, and then monitored by both the CDC and FDA. **Most adverse side-effects are minor and self-limited such as a local skin reaction or a mild temporary fever.**

Physicians should also remind parents that it is important to let other providers know of their child's vaccination status for any sick visit at other locations (e.g., urgent care clinics, emergency rooms) since being unvaccinated could add vaccine-preventable diseases on the provider's list of possible diagnoses.

DISMISSAL OF A FAMILY

Physicians should try their best to maintain a good relationship with parents and continue to educate them with each visit about vaccines. They should document any discussions about vaccines after each visit as well. **However, physicians do have the right to dismiss a family from their care** if shared goals are lacking, if there is mistrust, or if there is concern that the patient may spread a vaccine-preventable disease to other patients who are unable to be immunized due to a young age or medical contraindications. The physician should make sure to let the family know their clinic's policies about dismissing non-vaccinators and **help the family find another physician to transfer their care to.** The provider should continue to provide their patient care until the transition is complete.

ALTERNATIVE SCHEDULES

Physicians can offer an alternative vaccine schedule if all attempts have failed since an incomplete, or delayed, vaccination status is better than a completely unvaccinated status. Families should keep in mind that this may mean that their child will need to have more clinic visits to accommodate an alternative vaccine schedule.

REFERENCES
https://www.uptodate.com/contents/standard-childhood-vaccines-parental-hesitancy-or-refusal

Topic 31: Performance-Enhancing Drug Usage in Adolescent Athletes – Identifying
Identify an adolescent athlete who is using performance-enhancing drugs

BACKGROUND

Performance-enhancing drugs (PEDs) are used by adolescent athletes to improve their **athletic performance** and sometimes to improve their **physical appearance** as well. **Androgenic steroids** are the **most common type of PEDs**. They **increase lean body mass** and **decrease fat** composition. However, many **side-effects** occur from androgenic steroid use, and these can help to identify patients using them.

CARDIOVASCULAR SIDE EFFECTS

CARDIAC HYPERTROPHY

There have been several sporadic case reports of sudden deaths in adolescent athletes who were taking androgenic steroids and had no family history and no past medical history of sudden death. These case reports found the cause of death to be either **cardiac hypertrophy** or **myocarditis**. There have also been reports of **left ventricular hypertrophy**.

ABNORMAL LIPID PROFILES

Exogenous androgens can **decrease HDL** and **increase LDL**.

HEMATOLOGICAL SIDE EFFECTS

HEMOSTATIC SYSTEM ACTIVATION

Use of androgenic steroids can **activate the hemostatic system**, which can **increase** thrombin-antithrombin complexes, prothrombin fragment 1, **antithrombin III**, and **protein S**. It can also decrease tissue plasminogen activator and its inhibitor. It is unclear if this causes an increased incidence of thromboses.

ERYTHROPOIESIS

Exogenous testosterone and GnRH agonists can **increase hemoglobin and hematocrit** by stimulating **erythropoiesis**.

NEUROPYSCHIATRIC SIDE EFFECTS

PSYCHIATRIC SYMPTOMS

Androgenic steroids can increase the risk for **mood disorders** and **aggressive/violent behavior**. Females have also reported experiencing symptoms of **hypomania and depression**.

REPRODUCTIVE SIDE EFFECTS

FEMALES

Exogenous androgens in females can cause **acne, hirsutism**, male pattern **balding, clitoromegaly**, and a **deeper voice**.

MALES

Chronic use of exogenous androgens in males can cause **hypogonadism** due to prolonged gonadotropin suppression, which can result in **decreased spermatogenesis and fertility**. Exogenous testosterone can be aromatized into estradiol, which can result in **gynecomastia**.

OTHER SIDE EFFECTS

INFECTION

The process of **injecting** androgens increases the risk for infections such as **local abscesses** and **septic arthritis**. Sharing needles can also increase the risk for infections like **HIV**, **Hepatitis B**, and **Hepatitis C**.

TENDON RUPTURE

Triceps or biceps tendon rupture risk is increased with exogenous use of androgens.

EPIPHYSEAL CLOSURE

Exogenous testosterone can be aromatized to estradiol, which can cause **earlier epiphyseal closure** in those whose epiphyses have not closed yet.

HEPATIC

Only **oral 17-alpha-alkylated androgens** can cause hepatic side effects such as **elevated liver function enzymes** and **cholestatic jaundice**.

SIGNS OF SUSPECTED ANDROGEN USE

Physicians should consider performance-enhancing drug usage in adolescent athletes participating in **competitive sports** such as swimming, cycling, football, and baseball. The following can be signs of suspected androgen use:

- **Behavioral changes** such as **irritability, aggression**, and **depression**
- Rapid increase in **muscle strength and mass**
- **Acne**
- **Elevated hematocrit, low LH, low sex hormone binding globulin (SHBG)**
- **Males** with **hypogonadism, gynecomastia, decreased sperm count, or tendon ruptures**
- **Females** with **irregular menses, hirsutism, breast atrophy, temporal balding, clitoromegaly, and deepening of their voice**
- **Early puberty, premature epiphyseal closure**, and a final **height shorter** than predicted

REFERENCES

https://www.uptodate.com/contents/use-of-androgens-and-other-hormones-by-athletes

Topic 32: Polydactyly in Infants – Evaluating and Managing
Evaluate and manage an infant with polydactyly

BACKGROUND
Polydactyly refers to the presence of extra digits. The extra digit(s) can be present on one or more hands and feet. The extra digit is usually a small piece of soft tissue that can be removed. Occasionally, it contains bone without joints. Rarely it may be a complete, functioning digit.

EVALUATION

GENERAL
Polydactyly is **more common in the Black population** in the US. Preaxial polydactyly is more common amongst Whites, Native Americans, and Asians. Postaxial polydactyly occurs more frequently found in the Black population.

Prenatal ultrasounds can find polydactyly as early as 9 weeks gestational age. Upon discovery, clinicians should evaluate the rest of the extremities and should also look for additional congenital anomalies (e.g., cardiac, renal, nervous system, etc.).

Postnatal evaluation includes starting with an AP and lateral plain film x-ray. Confirm that there are no other associated anomalies which would suggest an associated disease.

UPPER EXTREMITY (HANDS)
- **PREAXIAL POLYDACTYLY (AKA RADIAL POLYDACTYLY)** refers to an extra thumb. These patients are more likely to have additional syndromes. This is the most common form of hand polydactyly.
- **POSTAXIAL POLYDACTYLY (AKA ULNAR POLYDACTYLY)** refers to an extra digit on the 5th digit (pinky finger). These patients are less likely to have additional syndrome.
- **CENTRAL POLYDACTYLY** refers to an extra digit located on one of the middle three digits. This can often be **associated with syndactyly and cleft hand.**

LOWER EXTREMITY (FEET)
- **TIBIAL POLYDACTYLY** refers to an extra digit at the first digit (big toe).
- **FIBULAR POLYDACTYLY** refers to polydactyly at the 5th digit (pinky toe).
- **CENTRAL POLYDACTYLY** refers to polydactyly at one of the middle 3 toes.

ASSOCIATIONS
In isolation, polydactyly may have an association with family history. However, polydactyly may be associated with certain syndromes:
- Trisomy 13
- Meckel syndrome
- Down syndrome
- Diamond-Blackfan anemia
- Bardet-Biedl syndrome
- Fanconi anemia
- Rubinstein-Taybi syndrome

- VACTERL (vertebral defects, anal atresia, cardiac defects, trachea esophageal fistula, renal anomalies, and limb abnormalities) association

MANAGEMENT

MANAGEMENT OF UPPER EXTREMITY POLYDACTYLY
The management depends on the complexity and location of the extra digit.
- **SUTURE LIGATION:** If there is NO bone/ligament within the extra digit, "suture ligation" may be performed. A suture can be tied tightly to cut off blood supply to the extra digit so that it may necrose and fall off.
- **ORTHOPEDICS REFERRAL:** If there is bone/ligament within the extra digit, refer to an orthopedic surgeon for surgical removal. Additionally, if there is preaxial/radial polydactyly (at the thumb) of the hand, this should be referred to orthopedics for surgical evaluation to ensure that the functioning thumb is not damaged.

MANAGEMENT OF LOWER EXTREMITY POLYDACTYLY
Due to special considerations around walking, cosmesis, and quality of life, any polydactyly of the foot should be referred to an orthopedic surgeon for evaluation and treatment.

REFERENCES

https://www.ncbi.nlm.nih.gov/books/NBK562295

Topic 33: Prenatally Diagnosed Hydronephrosis in Infants – Evaluating and Managing

Evaluate and manage an infant with prenatally diagnosed hydronephrosis

BACKGROUND

Genitourinary and kidney abnormalities are the most common abnormalities noted on routine screening **prenatal ultrasound**. Among these is **hydronephrosis** which is the dilation of the proximal urinary collecting system. Hydronephrosis is the most common abnormality identified, occurring in up to 0.6% of all prenatal ultrasounds.

EVALUATION

POSTNATAL ULTRASOUND

The start of the evaluation process after the infant is born includes obtaining a **postnatal ultrasound. If the infant is stable**, wait until 1 week of age to obtain the ultrasound. If there is concern of being able to follow up at 1 week, obtain at discharge and then again at 4-6 weeks of age. **If oliguric and unstable**, do not wait one week. Obtain at $\geq$ 48 hours after birth.

The results of the ultrasound are usually as follows:

- **50% of postnatal ultrasounds** demonstrate resolution of prenatal hydronephrosis
- **15% of postnatal ultrasounds** show persistent hydronephrosis that are not associated with urinary tract obstruction. They are referred to as "physiologic" or non-refluxing, non-obstructive hydronephrosis. Of these, only 10% will require surgery due to the development of obstruction. The rest will resolve entirely by age 3 years old.
- **35% of postnatal ultrasounds** and show obstructive or refluxing causes such as:
    - Ureteropelvic junction (UPJ) obstruction
    - Vesicoureteral reflux (VUR)
    - Posterior urethral valves (PUV)
    - Megaureter
    - Ureterocele

GRADING SEVERITY

The severity of hydronephrosis is based off measuring the anterior-posterior pelvic diameter.

- **< 10 mm**: Normal or mild hydronephrosis
- **10-15 mm**: Moderate hydronephrosis
- **> 15 mm**: Severe hydronephrosis

HISTORY & PHYSICAL EXAM

A good history and physical exam can help narrow down the diagnosis.

HISTORY OF VOIDING PATTERN

- Little to no urine (oligoanuria) within the first 48 hours after birth strongly suggests an obstructive lesion

PHSYICAL EXAM
- Palpable abdominal or flank mass (UPJ or multicystic, dysplastic kidney)
- Distended bladder (PUV or urethral stricture)
- Absent abdominal musculature and undescended testicles (Prune belly syndrome)

IMAGING STUDIES
VOIDING CYSTOURETHROGRAM (VCUG)
- Obtain if postnatal hydronephrosis is present on ultrasound to evaluate for VUR, ureterocele, urethral stricture, or PUV.

DIURETIC RENOGRAPHY (MAG-3)
- Obtain if postnatal hydronephrosis is present and UPJ (ureterovesical junction obstruction) is suspected.

MANAGEMENT

NORMAL OR MILD HYDRONEPHROSIS
No further evaluation is needed.

MODERATE HYDRONEPHROSIS
A repeat ultrasound at 4-6 months of age is recommended. At that time, manage based the results of th repeat ultrasound:
- **RESOLUTION OF HYDRONEPHROSIS:** No further management needed. Most resolve by 18 months of age.
- **NO CHANGE IN HYDRONEPHROSIS:** Continue to monitor with an ultrasound at 1 year of age, followed by 3-5 years of age if needed. Obtain diuretic renography (MAG-3) if symptomatic (pain with urination or increased urinary frequency) to look for an obstructive process.
- **INCREASING HYDRONEPHROSIS:** Obtain diuretic renography (MAG-3) to look for an obstructive process.

SEVERE HYDRONEPHROSIS
Obtain diuretic renography (MAG-3) at 6 weeks of age to look for possible obstruction after and refer to a pediatric urologist.

ANTIBIOTIC PROPHYLAXIS AND CIRCUMCISION
Antibiotic prophylaxis is controversial for hydronephrosis. Circumcision should not routinely be recommend for neonates with hydronephrosis as there is no evidence of negative renal outcomes in uncircumcised children with hydronephrosis. When used, **amoxicillin or cephalexin** is used in infants less than three months of age, and **trimethoprim-sulfamethoxazole (TMP-SMX) or nitrofurantoin** is used in children greater than three months of age. Generally, antibiotic prophylaxis is **not used in infants with low-grade or moderate grade hydronephrosis**. In the following circumstances, most centers would opt for providing antibiotic prophylaxis:
- Dilated ureters
- Enlarged bladder due to PUV
- Bilateral UPJ obstruction
- Giant hydronephrosis (RPD > 30 mm)

REFERENCES

https://www.uptodate.com/contents/fetal-hydronephrosis-postnatal-management
https://publications.aap.org/pediatricsinreview/article-abstract/32/12/e110/32853
https://publications.aap.org/neoreviews/article-abstract/14/11/e551/88391

Topic 34: Primary Immunodeficiency Disorders – Recognizing the Presentation
Recognize the presentation of primary immunodeficiency disorders

BACKGROUND
The term **primary immunodeficiency disorder (PID), also known as an inborn error of immunity, refers over 300 known genetic defects of the immune system**. The prevalence of PIDs is approximately 1 in 1,200 to 2,000 individuals. In general, **PIDs nearly universally result in more frequent, severe, or atypical infections**, though just 10% of children with recurrent infections are diagnosed with a PID.

The most severe, **life-threatening disorders usually present in infancy**, while the less severe disorders may not present until adulthood. **Some PIDs are associated with specific types of infections**. Others result in characteristic non-infectious signs and symptoms.

WHEN TO SUSPECT A PRIMARY IMMUNE DEFIENCY

NORMAL INFECTIOUS HISTORY IN A CHILD
To recognize abnormal patterns of infections, one must first understand what is normal. This includes:
- Approximately 4-8 respiratory infections per year
- Mean duration of viral respiratory illness of 8 days, with an individual episole lasting up to 2 weeks
- Less than 2 pneumonias and less than 3 uncomplicated acute otitis media infections in the first 3 years of life
- Normal growth curve

SIGNS ASSOCIATED WITH A PID IN INFANCY
- Hypocalcemia
- Conotruncal heart defects
- Absence of thymic shadow
- Delayed umbilical cord detachment >30 days

SIGNS ASSOCIATED WITH A PID IN A CHILD
- Family history of PID
- Recurrent Infections: $\geq$ 6 respiratory tract infections in 1 year, $\geq$ 4 episodes of AOM, $\geq$ 2 serious sinus infections or pneumonias, recurrent candidiasis, abscesses
- Atypical or severe infections: hospitalizations requiring IV antibiotics
- Chronic symptoms (chronic diarrhea, unexplained fevers)
- Complications from a live vaccines or vaccine failure (recurrent varicella infections in a vaccinated child)
- Failure to thrive
- Severe atopy or other extensive skin lesions
- Autoinflammatory or autoimmune disease (examples: HLH, lymphoma)

NON-IMMUNOLOGIC MANIFESTATIONS OF PIDs

Many PIDs have non-immunologic manifestations that can help to narrow the differential. These often reflect generalized underlying internal dysregulation including autoimmune and autoinflammatory conditions.

GI MANIFESTATIONS

- Chronic Enteropathy: T cell dysregulation
- Inflammatory Bowel Disease: Any autoimmune/immune dysregulation
- Multiple Intestinal Atresia: TTC7A deficiency

DERMATOLOGIC CONDITIONS

- Eczema: Hyper-IgE Syndrome, Wiskott-Aldrich
- Neutrophilic Pustular Dermatosis: Proteasome-associated autoinflammation
- Cutaneous Granulomas: CGD, ataxia-telangiectasia, Blau syndrome
- Hypopigmented Hair: Chédiak-Higashi syndrome
- Thin Hair: Dyskeratosis congenita
- Brittle "Bamboo" Hair: Comèl-Netherton syndrome
- Abnormal Skin Pigmentation: Dyskeratosis congenita, Chédiak-Higashi

AUTOIMMUNE MANIFESTATIONS

- Arthritis: Any hyperinflammatory condition
- Cytopenia: Periodic fever syndromes
- Vasculitis: Complement pathway defects, CGD
- SLE-Like Disease: STAT5B deficiency, ataxia-telangiectasia

ENDOCRINOPATHIES

- T1DM, Thyroid Disease, Hypoparathyroidism, Adrenal Insufficiency: immune tolerance dysregulation
- Growth Hormone Deficiency: DiGeorge, AIRE deficiency

HEME/ONC MANIFESTATIONS

- Lymphoproliferative Disease (EBV): Impaired activation and dysregulated proliferation of immune cells
- Hemophagocytic lymphohistiocytosis (HLH): Chédiak-Higashi, CGD, periodic fever syndromes

PULMONIC MANIFESTATIONS

- Interstitial Lung Disease, Pulmonary Alveolar Proteinosis, Eosinophilic Pneumonia: Impaired activation and dysregulated proliferation of immune cells

NEUROLOGIC MANIFESTATIONS

- Hearing Loss: Carnevale-Mingarelli-Malpuech-Michaels syndrome
- Developmental Delay: Ataxia-telangiectasia, Chédiak-Higashi

CATEGORIES OF PIDS

IMPAIRED HUMORAL IMMUNITY (B CELLS)

There is impaired antibody production which is essential for protection of the sinopulmonary tract. The typical **age of presentation is approximately 3-4 months** due to the waning of maternal protection around this time. An example includes **X-linked agammaglobulinemia** which is characterized by a lack of B cells and resultant lack in antibody production. These may be suspected because of:

- **Frequent sinopulmonary tract infections**: acute otitis media, sinusitis, pneumonia
- **Infections with encapsulated bacteria**: Strep pneumoniae, Haemophilus influenzae
- **Other Infections**: Salmonella, Campylobacter, Giardia, rotavirus, mycoplasma, pseudomonas

IMPAIRED T-CELL DEFICIENCY

There are defects of cellular and humoral immunity. Severe combined immunodeficiency disorder (SCID) is an example which is detected on the newborn screen. T-cell deficiencies may be suspected due to:

- **Same infections as humoral immune dysfunction and more**
- **Opportunistic Infections**: Candida, PJP, Mycobacteria, Cryptosporidium
- **Life-threatening viral infection**: RSV, rhinovirus, parainfluenza, adenovirus, CMV, live vaccines
- **Failure to thrive**

PHAGOCYTIC DEFECTS

Phagocytic defects result in **impaired neutrophils** (number or function) thus **impaired clearance of bacterial and fungal pathogens**. Chronic granulomatous disease (CGD) is an exam. These may be suspected due to:

- **Bacterial and fungal infections**
- **Abscesses of skin or organs**
- **Cellulitis, pneumonia, gingival disease, aphthous stomatitis**
- **Omphalitis**
- **Poor wound healing**
- **Severe Staph aureus, Pseudomonas aeruginosa infections**
- **CGD specific problems**: infections with catalase-positive organisms (S. aureus, **Serratia**, Klebsiella, Burkholderia, Aspergillus, Nocardia) or complications of the BCG vaccine

COMPLEMENT DEFICIENCIES

Complement-related PIDs are divided into early or terminal pathway defects. These may be suspected due to:

- **Early pathway defects** resulting in infections by **encapsulated bacteria** (S pneumoniae, H influenzae).
- **Terminal pathway defects** resulting in sepsis or meningitis due to **Neisseria meningitidis**.

IDENTIFY SPECIFIC PIDs by CORRESPONDING ONSET & SYMPTOMS

PIDs BY AGE OF ONSET

Some PIDs have a characteristic age of onset that is related to the underlying etiology. **Maternal immunoglobulin protection (IgG) wanes between 4 and 7 months**, thus PIDs often present within the first year. **Less severe PIDs tend to present after 2 years of age.**

0 - 6 months	Congenital neutropenia Leukocyte Adhesion Defects Toll-Like Receptor Defects – specifically HSV encephalitis Complement Deficiencies DiGeorge Syndrome
6 months – 2 years	Congenital antibody deficiencies Combined immunodeficiencies – very early onset IBD, CD25 def.
2 - 6 years	Less severe congenital antibody deficiencies -- IgA deficiency, selective ab deficiencies Less severe combined immunodeficiencies -- ataxia-telangiectasia, cartilage-hair hypoplasia
6 - 18 years	Less severe complement deficiencies, CVID, autoimmune or autoinflammatory disease

PIDs BY CHARACTERISTIC INFECTION

Some PIDs have characteristic infectious organisms that may help to signal a PID is present and identify the underlying disorder.

Recurrent URI with encapsulated organisms (pneumococcus, haemophilus influenzae B)	Humoral/B Cell Deficiencies
Recurrent pneumococcal disease	Complement defect, Agammaglobulinemia
PJP	CD40 ligand deficiency, T-cell deficiencies including SCID
Pseudomonas sepsis	Phagocytic disorders, Humoral / B Cell Deficiency, Abnormal T cell immunity
Enteroviral meningoencephalitis	X-linked agammaglobulinemia
Abscesses containing Aspergillus, Staph aureus, coagulase-negative staph, Serratia marcescens	CGD
Recurrent staph skin infections, abscesses, lung cysts, pneumonia	Hyperimmunoglobulin E syndrome
Severe Candidiasis	Abnormal T cell immunity
Invasive Neisseria	Complement deficiency (late components)
Infection following a live vaccine	Abnormal T cell immunity
Severe non-TB mycobacteria infection	Defective pathways of interferon-gamma or IL-12

SYNDROMIC PIDS

Some PIDs have characteristic signs unrelated to the immune defect. In addition to abnormal susceptibilities to infection, syndromic PIDs may be identified by their unique features.

Ataxia, telangiectasia, developmental delay	Ataxia-telangiectasia
Petechiae, bleeding, eczema, ear drainage	Wiskott-Aldrich
Coarse features, chronic eczema, abscesses, scoliosis	Hyperimmunoglobulin E
Short stature, metaphyseal dystrophy, fine hair	Cartilage-hair hypoplasia
Congenital heart disease, developmental delay, low-set ears, dysmorphic facies	DiGeorge
Seborrheic dermatitis, alopecia	SCID
Oral ulcers, gingivitis, impetigo	CGD, Leukocyte-Adhesion defects
Oculocutaneous albinism	Chediak-Higashi
Abnormal dentition, decreased sweating, sparse hair	Ectodermal dysplasia
Dermatomyositis	XLA
Lupus-like rash	Complement component defects (early)
Warts, molluscum	T cell disorders, innate defects

REFERENCES
https://publications.aap.org/pediatricsinreview/article/40/5/229/35282

https://www.uptodate.com/contents/primary-immunodeficiency-overview-of-management

Topic 35: Rheumatic Fever – Recognizing the Clinical Features
Recognize the clinical features of rheumatic fever

BACKGROUND
Rheumatic fever is caused by Group A Streptococcus (GAS, AKA Strep PYOGENES) infection and is almost always due to a **PHARYNGITIS**. Rarely, though, it may be caused by **Scarlet fever**. It is not associated with skin infections.

JONES CRITERIA FOR RHEUMATIC FEVER
The Jones criteria were created to help diagnose rheumatic fever. There are **major and minor criteria**. There are **three ways to use these criteria to diagnose rheumatic fever**, and they include the:
- Patient meeting **2 of the MAJOR** Jones criteria.
- Patient meeting **1 major AND 2 minor** Jones criteria.
- Patients having a previous **history of** acute rheumatic fever (ARF) or rheumatic heart disease **and meeting 3 minor criteria.**

Note that evidence of a previous Group A Strep infection is required in any of the above 3 scenarios. AVOID ordering a Streptococcal screen or culture since these can be positive in carriers and since they can be negative in a recently resolved pharyngitis. Instead, order ASO titers or Streptozyme, which correlate better with recent infection. In some cases, a presumptive diagnosis of acute rheumatic fever can be made without fulfilling the Jones Criteria such as in areas with high acute rheumatic fever incidence.

PEARL: Joint criteria can only be used once, so you cannot use arthritis as a major criterion and also use arthralgia as a minor criterion.

PEARL: **EXCEPTIONS** to JONES Criteria include **CHOREA alone**, in the context of a recent Strep infection, may be diagnostic. Also, "indolent" **carditis** (i.e. not acute) may be the only manifestation months after a Strep infection.

MAJOR JONES CRITERIA FOR ACUTE RHEUMATIC FEVER
Major Jones Criteria for acute rheumatic fever include:
- An asymmetric, migratory, **polyarthritis** of the large joints (ankles, knees, wrists)
- Signs of **carditis**: Valves, myocardium, and pericardium can be affected so look for new murmurs, CHF, cardiomegaly, and pericarditis.
- Painless, firm subcutaneous **nodules** (wrists, elbows, knees)
- **ERYTHEMA MARGINATUM**
  - Erythema marginatum is a transient, erythematous, macular and light colored. It is described as being "SERPENTiginous" (snakelike) and the **MARGIN**s are noted progress as the center clears. It is part of the Jones criteria for Rheumatic Fever.
  - **IMAGE**: www.pbrlinks.com/ERYTHEMA1
- **Sydenham's Chorea**: Movements of the face and/or extremities without purpose. Some describe it as "purposeless dancing."

MNEMONIC for the MAJOR JONES CRITERIA:

- "J O N E S" is a mnemonic to help you remember the major Jones criteria:
- **J**oints: asymmetric, migratory, polyarthritis of the large joints (ankles, knees, wrists)
- **O** looks like a HEART: Carditis = new murmurs, CHF, cardiomegaly and pericarditis.
- **N**odules: Painless and firm subcutaneous nodules (wrists, elbows, knees)
- **E**rythema **MARGIN**atum: The name **MARGIN**atum should remind you of the interesting facts regarding the MARGINs of the rash.
- **S**ydenham's Chorea: Movements of the face and/or extremities without purpose and sometimes described as "purposeless dancing."

MINOR JONES CRITERIA FOR ACUTE RHEUMATIC FEVER

Minor Jones criteria for acute rheumatic fever include:

- ARTHRALGIAS: Refers to pain **without inflammation**. Note that this is a MINOR criterion.
- ESR OR CRP elevation
- FEVER
- PR INTERVAL prolongation

RHEUMATIC FEVER ASSOCIATIONS

- **Aschoff bodies** are nodules on the heart or in the aorta. They are **pathognomonic for Acute Rheumatic Fever**. Biopsy reveals inflammatory cells arranged in a "ROSETTE" pattern around a fibrinoid core.
- **Valvular dysfunction** is common, including mitral, tricuspid, and aortic valve defects. Lesions can be stenotic or due to regurgitation. Mitral stenosis and tricuspid stenosis are frequently due to rheumatic fever. Mitral regurgitation is the most common murmur of rheumatic fever. Possible descriptions might include the harsh, systolic, apical murmur of mitral regurgitation, or the apical diastolic murmur of aortic regurgitation (so look for evidence of **congestive heart failure**).
- **Endocarditis** occurs due to destruction of valves, NOT infection.
- **Emotional lability, dysarthria, hypotonia, tics, OCD, ADD, and anxiety** are associated with Sydenham chorea

REFERENCES

https://www.uptodate.com/contents/acute-rheumatic-fever-clinical-manifestations-and-diagnosis
https://publications.aap.org/pediatricsinreview/article-abstract/42/5/221/180705
https://www.cdc.gov/groupastrep/diseases-hcp/acute-rheumatic-fever.html

Topic 36: Safety and Injury Prevention for School-Age Children (Ages 5-10 Years) – Providing Anticipatory Guidance

Provide anticipatory guidance regarding safety and injury prevention for school-age children (ages 5 to 10 years)

BACKGROUND
The anticipatory guidance regarding safety and injury prevention for school-age children varies by age. The recommendations are from Bright Futures and broken up by age group starting with ages 5-6 years old, followed by 7-8 years old, and finally 9-10 years old.

AGES 5 AND 6 YEARS OLD
Educate families on the importance of gun locks, safety belt/booster seats, safety helmets, swimming safety, fire escape/drills, child sexual abuse prevention, smoke detectors, and CO2 detectors. More details provided below:
- Remove guns from home.
- If guns are stored in the home, store them unloaded and locked with the ammunition locked separately.
- Use a booster seat with proper belt-positioning in back seat.
- Use safety equipment with sports (pads, helmet, eye protection).
- Provide swimming lessons, use sunscreen, use a fence around pools, and supervise the child around water.
- Install smoke/carbon dioxide detectors and make a fire escape plan.
- Educate on safe street habits (crossing the street and riding the school bus).
- Provide rules that allow for safety around adults:
    - No adult should tell a child to keep secrets from their parents
    - No adult should express interest in a child's private parts
    - No adult should ask a child for help with his/her private parts

AGES 7 AND 8 YEARS OLD
Educate families on the importance of knowing the child's friends/family, supervising with friends, safety belts/booster seats, helmets, playground safety, sports safety, swimming safety, sunscreen, smoke-free home/car, gun safety, and careful monitoring of computer use (games, internet, email, and social media). More details are provided below:
- Know child's friends/family members
- Teach rules to be safe around adults
- Use belt-positioning booster seat in back seat until lap/shoulder belt fits
- Safety equipment with sports
- Swimming lessons, use of sunscreen, and proper supervision around water
- Keep home/car smoke-free
- Teach home safety rules for fire/emergencies
- Remove guns from home
- If guns are stored in the home, store them unloaded and locked with the ammunition locked separately.
- Monitor computer/TV/phone use and install safety apps and parental preferences

AGES 9 AND 10 YEARS OLD

Educate families on the importance of gun locks, safety belts, helmets, bicycle safety, swimming, sunscreen, tobacco/alcohol/drugs, knowing child's friends/family, supervision of child with friends, and supervision of electronics. More details provided below:

- Remove guns from home
- If guns are stored in the home, store them unloaded and locked with the ammunition locked separately.
- Back seat is the safest place to ride and keep the child in a booster seat until 4'9" tall, then can use the safety belt in rear seat without a booster seat
- Safety equipment with sports (pads, helmet, eye protection)
- Swimming lessons, use of sunscreen, and supervise around water
- Counsel about avoiding tobacco, alcohol, and drugs
- Know child's friends and make plan for personal safety
- Monitor computer/TV/phone use and install safety apps and parental preferences

REFERENCES

https://downloads.aap.org/AAP/PDF/Bright%20Futures/BF4_POCKETGUIDE.pdf
https://downloads.aap.org/AAP/PDF/BF_SafetyInjuryPrev_Tipsheet.pdf
https://publications.aap.org/aapbooks/monograph/478/chapter-abstract/5801068

Topic 37: SARS-CoV-2 Infection in Children – Recognizing the Clinical Manifestations (including Post-Acute Sequelae) and Planning Appropriate Initial Evaluation or Management

Recognize the clinical manifestations of SARS-CoV-2 infection in children (including post-acute sequelae) and plan appropriate initial evaluation/management

BACKGROUND

The SARS-CoV-2 infection that causes COVID-19 in children has a wide range of clinical manifestations from having no symptoms at all to life-threatening or even fatal outcomes. **Most commonly, children are asymptomatic.** Patients who have symptoms usually recovered within 1-2 weeks.

CLINICAL MANIFESTATIONS

SYMPTOMS

The most common symptoms of COVID-19 in children are fever, cough, sore throat, headache, shortness of breath, rhinorrhea, myalgia, abdominal pain, nausea, vomiting, diarrhea, and a loss of taste or smell (which can present as food refusal in children who are nonverbal). **Other less common clinical manifestations include** neurological problems like seizures (febrile and nonfebrile) and encephalopathy and dermatological problems (e.g., maculopapular or urticarial rashes), cardiovascular problems (e.g., myocarditis), and renal problems (e.g., acute kidney injury). Of note, hyperglycemia and leukopenia were seen in preterm infants.

COMPLICATIONS

MULTISYSTEM INFLAMMATORY SYNDROME IN CHILDREN (MIS-C)

Although it is rare, MIS-C is a serious complication of COVID-19 infection in children. MIS-C symptoms include persistent fever, rash, hypotension, myocarditis, GI symptoms, and elevated inflammatory markers. These features are **similar to Kawasaki disease and toxic shock syndrome**, and therefore they must be further evaluated and differentiated to ensure proper management and treatment.

LONG COVID

Long covid is used to describe any post-COVID 19 conditions that either persistently remain, reoccur, or even manifest as new symptoms that affected the physical or mental health of the patient for **at least 12 weeks** after the initial confirmed infection, cannot be explained by another diagnosis, and affects daily functioning. **The most common long covid symptoms include** an altered sense of smell or taste, fatigue, sleep disturbance, headache, muscle and joint pain, weakness, respiratory issues, and palpitations.

GENERAL MANAGEMENT

Although there were initially concerns about the safety of using NSAIDS, ACE-inhibitors, and ARBs for patients with COVID-19, studies showed that there were no significant adverse associations. Therefore, these medications can be continued for patients who do not have any other contraindications.

OUTPATIENT MANAGEMENT

Most patients with mild symptoms can be treated at home as outpatients with supportive care. Parents should be counseled on monitoring their child's symptoms to look for any signs of deterioration that should prompt a visit to either the urgent care or ER. **Red flag symptoms include** severe respiratory distress, cyanosis, difficulty breathing, chest pain, inability to take PO liquids, and having any signs of shock, such as decreased urine output, difficulty arousing, mottled skin, cold and clammy skin, or altered mental status. If the patient has mild to moderate symptoms but has a high risk of progressing to severe symptoms, outpatient antiviral therapy can be considered on a case-by-case basis if started within 5-7 days of symptom onset. Examples of outpatient therapies include antiviral medications such as PO nirmatrelvir-ritonavir and IV remdesivir. **Monoclonal antibodies are no longer provided as an outpatient therapy.**

INPATIENT MANAGEMENT

HOSPITALIZATON CRITERIA

Patients infected with COVID-19 with the following symptoms should be admitted to the hospital if they any of the following:

- Lower respiratory disease that is either severe or critical
- Underlying disease that increases the risk of severe disease (e.g., immunodeficiency)
- Fever in a patient less than 30 days of age

MANAGEMENT

All children with COVID-19 should receive supportive care. **Supportive care may include** respiratory support (oxygen or ventilation support), fluids, electrolyte support, empiric antibiotics as indicated if the patient acquires a bacterial infection (e.g., pneumonia), monitoring of labs (CRP, D-dimer, ferritin, and LDH) to look for cytokine release syndrome, and thromboprophylaxis in the form of pneumatic compression or early mobility.

ANTIVIRAL THERAPY

Antiviral therapy should only be done on a case-by-case basis and preferably in a clinical trial at this time. Although the benefits have not been proven yet, antiviral therapy is recommended in children who have severe or critical COVID-19, or are at risk of severe disease (e.g., immunocompromised, medically complex, or have congenital heart disease). **The most common antiviral drug used against COVID-19 is remdesivir**, which is a nucleotide analog that inhibits RNA-dependent RNA polymerase. Remdesivir can reduce the child's recovery time of their COVID-19 symptoms.

REFERENCES

https://www.uptodate.com/contents/covid-19-clinical-manifestations-and-diagnosis-in-children
https://www.uptodate.com/contents/covid-19-management-in-children

Topic 38: Self-Injurious Behavior in Adolescents – Managing
Manage an adolescent with self-injurious behavior

BACKGROUND
Self-injurious behavior is purposeful destruction of one's body tissue, which can include cutting one's skin, burning themselves, or severely scratching oneself. Most patients with self-injurious behavior do not seek treatment. Adolescents have the highest rates of self-injurious behaviors, and these behaviors are associated with suicidal attempts. Screening for suicidal ideation should be done with the patient alone (i.e., without guardians) since this may help the patient feel more comfortable opening up and disclosing any self-injurious behavior or suicidal ideations.

MANAGEMENT OF SELF-INJURIOUS BEHAVIORS

INDICATIONS FOR TREATMENT
- Multiple episodes
- A single episode used as a coping mechanism for significant distress
- Any episode that is medically serious (cutting) or requires medical attention (sutures)

TREATMENT SETTINGS & PERSONNEL
- **Outpatient treatment** is appropriate for those who are at **low risk for suicide.**
- **Inpatient hospitalization** may be indicated if a patient caused severe bodily harm that requires **medical interventions, cannot be monitored at home**, are at **high risk of suicide**, or have other **co-occurring psychiatric symptoms that may be a safety risk**.
- **Treat comorbid psychiatric disorders** such as anxiety, depression, and substance abuse disorders through referrals to the appropriate mental health professionals.
- **Coordinate care with the treatment team**, which could consist of a therapist, psychiatrist, social worker, teachers, and school counselors.

SPECIFIC TYPES OF THERAPY
Therapy helps to educate the patient, discuss motivation for treatment, identify triggers, and teach new coping skills and behaviors to replace self-injurious behaviors.

FIRST-LINE TREATMENT
Dialectical Behavior Therapy (DBT): includes group and individual therapy to reduce self-harming behaviors, address individual concerns, and help individuals use the skills they learned in group therapy.

SECOND-LINE TREATMENT
Cognitive Behavioral Therapy (CBT): teaches alternative coping skills and behavioral changes via cognitive restructuring by identifying maladaptive thoughts and focusing on more self-awareness.

THIRD-LINE TREATMENT
Other forms of psychotherapy such as family therapy, emotion regulation group therapy or interpersonal psychotherapy may be helpful.

MOTIVATIONAL INTERVIEWING

Suggested topics for sessions include physical, psychological, and social consequences, pros and cons of self-injury, meaning of self-injury, patient's life goals, motivations for stopping, barriers towards stopping, or discrepancy between the patient's current and future state.

FAMILY INVOLVEMENT AND CONFIDENTIALITY

Confidentiality issues may arise. The decision to honor or break confidentiality to involve the family or guardian is up to the **clinician's judgement regarding the patient's risk of harm to themselves**, which can include factors such as: frequency of behavior, methods used, medical severity, amount of distress causing such behaviors, amount of functional impairment, presence of suicidal ideation, or other psychopathologies. Discuss with the patient how the information should be discussed with their guardian to maintain good rapport.

Inform the guardian if the self-injurious behaviors are increasing in frequency or severity, co-occurring with suicidal thoughts or behaviors, or the patient's safety is at risk.
If **social media or peers** seems to be influencing these behaviors, limiting access should be discussed with guardians.

SAFETY PLAN

Clinicians and patients should come up with an **individualized safety plan** together. Safety plans should include a list of:

- What constitutes maintaining a safe environment.
- Warning signs or triggers
- Alternative strategies for coping (e.g., exercising, music, journaling, or reading)
- Resources that patient can utilize for support (e.g., family, friends, and mental health services)

Please note that safety contracts are not recommended.

EXPECTATIONS FOR TREATMENT

Recovery is a process, but success can be measured with **reduced frequency and severity** of self-injury and **using other coping skills** that are not self-injurious. To help monitor frequency and progress, patients should be asked to keep a daily or weekly log of their self-injurious behaviors, triggers, consequences, and any use of alternative coping skills when urges arise.

CLINICIAN'S ATTITUDE

Clinicians should be careful not to show judgement or negative attitudes, since this may cause patients to discontinue treatment or be reluctant to disclose any future self-injurious behaviors.

REFERENCES

https://www.uptodate.com/contents/nonsuicidal-self-injury-in-children-and-adolescents-prevention-and-choosing-treatment
https://www.uptodate.com/contents/nonsuicidal-self-injury-in-children-and-adolescents-general-principles-of-treatment
https://www.uptodate.com/contents/suicidal-ideation-and-behavior-in-children-and-adolescents-evaluation-and-management

Topic 39: Sexually Transmitted Infection Testing in Prepubertal and Peripubertal Children – Recognizing Indications

Recognize indications for sexually transmitted infection testing in prepubertal and peripubertal children

BACKGROUND

Physicians should suspect **sexual abuse** in children if they notice an **unusual pattern** in **the child's injury or behavior**. Most sexual abuse in children occurs in the **prepubertal and peripubertal** years. Although girls are more likely to be victims of sexual abuse, boys are less likely to report being a victim. **STDs** are prevalent in about **5-8% of pediatric sexual abuse victims**. Any case of suspected sexual abuse should be reported to **child protective services**.

PREPUBERTAL CHILDREN

INDICATIONS FOR STD SCREENING

Physicians should consider **screening for STDs** in **prepubertal children** if:

- The interview suggests that **sexual abuse** is a high likelihood.
- The suspected **sexual abuser** is a **stranger**.
- There are clinical signs or **symptoms of STD**.
- The patient has already been diagnosed with an **STD before**.
- The patient's sibling, or other close friend/family member, who is also a **child** was diagnosed with an **STD**.
- The suspected **sexual abuser** has an **STD** or is at high risk of having an STD.
- There is evidence of penetration in either the **genitals or anus**.
- There is evidence of **ejaculation** (semen).
- The patient lives in an area with a **high rate of STDs**.
- The **patient or guardian requests STD screening**.

POSTPUBERTAL ADOLESCENTS

INDICATIONS FOR STD SCREENING

There is **controversy** around whether to screen for STDs in **postpubertal adolescents** who have been **sexually active**. However, since STDs can be **asymptomatic**, it may be beneficial for the patient to get screened for STDs in case **treatment** is required. As a result, STD screening for postpubertal adolescents should be considered on a **case-by-case basis**.

PHYSICAL EXAM FINDINGS SUSPICIOUS FOR SEXUAL ABUSE

Physicians should **consider STD screening** if they note any of the following physical exam findings:

- **Genital discharge**
- **Injuries** in the **genital or anorectal** area that requires **surgery**
- A **hymen** with a **deep notch** in the posterior/inferior rim
- A **hymen** with a **thin posterior rim**
- A **hymen** with a **wide orifice**
- Any lesions that look like **genital warts**
- Any **ulcers or vesicular lesions** in the **anogenital** area
- **Significant anal dilation** of 2 cm or more

DIFFERENTIAL DIAGNOSIS FOR SEXUAL ABUSE

INJURIES
Injuries to the perineum or genitalia can occur **unintentionally**, including those seen with **straddle injuries**, entrapment with a clothing **zipper**, **hair tourniquets**, and **motor vehicle accidents.**

INFECTIONS
Erythema or inflammation of the perineum can be caused by other infections that are not sexually transmitted such as **strep vaginitis**, **candida**, **varicella**, **perianal cellulitis**, **pinworms**, and autoinoculation of **molluscum contagiosum.**

SKIN CONDITIONS
Erythema, bleeding, ulcers, and friability of the perineum can occur due to many different **dermatological conditions** such as **nonspecific vulvovaginitis** (from either **poor hygiene** or taking **bubble baths**), seborrheic dermatitis, **atopic dermatitis**, **contact dermatitis** such as from diapers**, lichen sclerosis**, lichen simplex, lichen planus, psoriasis, bullous pemphigoid, **Behcet syndrome**, hemangiomas in the perineal area, and **congenital dermal melanocytosis.**

ANAL CONDITIONS
Perianal bleeding or **bruising** can be due to diagnoses such as **hemorrhoids, Crohn's disease, rectal prolapse**, hemolytic uremic syndrome, and rectal tumors. **Perianal erythema** can be due to **encopresis, poor hygiene**, and **infections** that are not sexually transmitted.

URETHRAL CONDITIONS
Urethral conditions to consider include **urethral prolapse**, **ureteroceles**, **sarcoma botryoides**, and **caruncles.**

PATHOGENS INCLUDED IN STD SCREENING

GONORRHEA, CHLAMYDIA, TRICHOMONAS, BACTERIAL VAGINOSIS, AND BACTERIAL VAGINOSIS
STD screening should include testing for **gonorrhea, chlamydia, trichomonas,** and **bacterial vaginosis**. If the patient did not receive prophylactic antibiotics for these pathogens after an acute event, STD screening should be done **two weeks after an event** occurred since this is the **incubation time** for these pathogens.

HIV AND SYPHILIS
HIV and syphilis screening should also be **included** when STDs are being screened for, however the physician should keep in mind the possibility of **vertical transmission** for **HIV**. HIV and syphilis screening should both be done at the **initial visit after an acute event**, then repeated at **6 and 12 weeks** after the event occurred. HIV would require an additional repeated screen at **24 weeks**, but syphilis would not.

HEPATITIS B
The **hepatitis B surface antibody** should be tested for in the **pediatric patient** if they have **not completed** all three doses of their **HBV vaccine course**. If possible, the **suspected abuser** should be tested for the **hepatitis B surface antigen.**

OTHER

Other **less common pathogens** that can be included are lesions suggestive of **herpes simplex virus** (HSV), **human papilloma virus** (HPV), and **pediculosis pubis** which can be identified with the naked eye or a magnifying glass showing the **pubic lice, their eggs, or nymphs.**

REFERENCES

https://www.uptodate.com/contents/evaluation-of-sexual-abuse-in-children-and-adolescents

Topic 40: Short Stature in Children – Evaluating
Evaluate a child with short stature

BACKGROUND
There are many potential causes of short stature, and the most common causes are genetic short stature (aka familial short stature) and constitutional growth delay. Pathological causes must be considered as part of the evaluation and differential diagnosis process. In this topic we will cover the evaluation of a child with short stature.

EVALUATING SHORT STATURE

IDENTIFYING SHORT STATURE
Short stature is defined as a **height less than 2 standard deviations below the mean height for age and sex, or a height < 3rd percentile for age and sex**. Heights and weights should be accurately measured and plotted on a growth chart. In children < 2 years, length should be measured lying down. Once a child has been identified as having short stature, additional components of the evaluation process may begin, which may include:
- History and physical exam
- Assessment of the child growth velocity
- Calculation of the mid-parental height
- Radiological evaluations
- Laboratory evaluations
- Genetic evaluations

HISTORY AND PHYSICAL EXAM
Ask about the child's perinatal history, including whether the child was born **small for gestational age** or had a **history of neonatal hypoglycemia**. Review the current medication list since **chronic use of stimulant medications and glucocorticoid medications** can suppress growth.

On exam, if growth hormone deficiency exists you may note a **high-pitched voice and immature facial features**, or even **midline defects** if there is a pituitary problem. Congenital growth hormone deficiency is associated with **micropenis** is associated. Turner syndrome is associated with **low set ears, a webbed neck, increased carrying angle, and Madelung deformity**. Patients with hypothyroidism may have a **goiter**.

GROWTH VELOCITY
Children with pathologic causes of short stature are more likely to grow with an abnormally slow growth velocity. Ideally, the growth velocity can be calculated from height measurements at least 6 months apart, but having height measurements separated by a year or more is better.

NORMAL GROWTH
Intrauterine growth depends more on maternal nutrition and intrauterine factors. Growth during the first 2 years of life is very rapid, about 30 - 35 cm in total. Height measurements often cross percentile channels during the first 2 years of life as children move from their birth length (which depends on intrauterine factors) to the height percentile of their genetic potential. Then, between ages 2 - 3 and puberty, children grow at a relatively constant rate, about 5-6 cm/year. Girls have their growth spurt

early in their pubertal development (peak growth velocity 8 - 10 cm/year), and boys have their growth spurt late in puberty, reaching a peak growth velocity of about 10 cm/year. Girls on average stop growing at age 14, and boys typically reach their final height at about 16-17.

ABNORMALLY SLOW GROWTH
- Age 2 – 4 years: Less than 5.5 cm/year
- Age 4 – 6 years: Less than 5 cm/year
- Age 6 years – puberty: Less than 4 cm/year for boys, and less than 4.5 cm/year for girls

MID-PARENTAL TARGET HEIGHT
Calculate the mid-parental target height to get a sense of the genetic height potential of the child, keeping in mind that a parent may have experienced some factor, such as malnutrition, or chronic medications while growing up, which may have adversely affected their growth. If that is the case, then the mid-parental target height is not reliable. Take it with a grain of salt. **To calculate the mid-parental target height**, average the parents' heights together, then add or subtract 5 inches (or 13 cm) depending on whether the patient is a boy or a girl.

RADIOLOGICAL EVALUATION
Obtain a **bone age x-ray**, which is just an x-ray of the patient's left hand. A discrepancy of up to 2 years between a patient's bone age and their actual age is normal. Patients who have short stature due to constitutional delay have bone ages of ≥ 2 years younger.

LABORATORY EVALUATION
It is important to screen for chronic diseases that may affect growth, so include CBC, CMP, urinalysis, sed rate, and screening testing for celiac disease, which may include total IgA levels and tissue transglutaminase antibody levels. Hypothyroidism is important to rule out, so include free T4 and TSH. Screening for growth hormone deficiency includes testing IGF-1 and IGF-BP3 levels.

GENETIC EVALUATION
Every female patient being evaluated for short stature must have a karyotype done to rule out Turner syndrome. Female patients with mosaic Turner syndrome may not have any other physical exam findings apart from short stature. If the patient has disproportionate short stature (relatively short limbs for the length of their trunk), consider genetic testing for SHOX deficiency or common types of skeletal dysplasias such as achondroplasia or hypochondroplasia.

COMMON CAUSES OF SHORT STATURE

GENETIC (OR FAMILIAL) SHORT STATURE
These patients are born with a normal birth length, then downwardly cross percentile channels until they reach their genetically determined percentile at about age 2, then grow with a normal growth velocity. The bone age is typically neither advanced nor delayed, and puberty starts at a normal time.

CONSTITUTIONAL DELAY OF GROWTH AND PUBERTY
These patients also are born with a normal birth length and cross percentile channels initially. They also grow with a normal growth velocity from age 2 or 3 years until puberty. These patients have delayed bone ages, and they start puberty late. They reach their final height later than their classmates, and they reach a final height appropriate for their genetic potential.

HYPOTHYROIDISM

These patients grow normally until hypothyroidism develops, and then grow with an abnormally slow growth velocity. They may have symptoms of fatigue, constipation, dry skin, dry hair, and cold intolerance. A bone age will be delayed.

GROWTH HORMONE DEFICIENCY

If patients are born with growth hormone deficiency, they may have associated findings of midline defects, micropenis, a visual impairment, neonatal hypoglycemia, and hyperbilirubinemia (especially direct hyperbilirubinemia). Other pituitary hormone levels may also be abnormal. If the growth hormone deficiency develops later during childhood, the growth velocity will initially be normal, and then slow down after the growth hormone deficiency develops. Look for causes of acquired growth hormone deficiency by ordering an MRI +/- contrast with special attention to the pituitary gland.

CELIAC DISEASE, MALABSORPTION, OR INADEQUATE CALORIC INTAKE

These patients tend to be underweight. A review of the growth charts initially show loss of weight followed by a slowing of the growth velocity. In the case of celiac disease or inflammatory bowel disease, they also typically complain of abdominal pain, bloating, and have abnormal bowel movements.

TURNER SYNDROME

Girls with Turner syndrome have short stature and pubertal delay, and may have low set ears, webbed neck, high arched palate, "shield chest" because of their relatively short limbs, increased carrying angle, and Madelung deformity of the wrists. They tend to have challenges with executive functioning and visual spatial skills, so there may be struggles in school. There is potential heart disease and kidney disease as well.

REFERENCES

https://www.uptodate.com/contents/diagnostic-approach-to-children-and-adolescents-with-short-stature

Topic 41: Sickle Cell Disease Complications: Understanding the Prevention and Management

Understand the prevention and management of complications of sickle cell disease

BACKGROUND

Patients with sickle cell disease (SCD) can have a variable range in symptoms and symptom severity. **Acute complications of SCD include** infections, severe anemia, and vaso-occlusive problems. **Although there are many chronic complications of SCD, the most common are pain and anemia.**

INFECTIONS

Functional hyposplenism and asplenism occurs in children with SCD, therefore they are at a higher risk of infections (especially with encapsulated organisms and viruses). Other reasons why children with SCD are at higher risk of infections include:

- Altered cellular and humoral immunity
- Hypoventilation
- Reduced tissue perfusion
- Splinting
- Presence of indwelling catheters

COMMON PATHOGENS

Malaria is a common cause of morbidity and mortality for children with SCD worldwide. **Patients with SCD are more susceptible to infections by encapsulated organisms such as S. pneumoniae and H. influenzae, which can cause bacteremia and meningitis.** Other causes of bacteremia include E. coli, S. aureus, and Salmonella species. Mycoplasma and Chlamydia pneumoniae are common causes of pneumonia and acute chest syndrome (ACS).

PREVENTIVE CARE

Parents should be counseled extensively on preventive care for children with SCD. **If their child develops a fever or other signs of infection**, they should seek immediate medical evaluation to initiate proper treatment as soon as possible. **Information about prophylactic penicillin and vaccines against encapsulated organisms (e.g., pneumococci and H. influenzae)** should also be included in the anticipatory guidance for parents.

ANEMIA

CHRONIC COMPENSATED HEMOLYTIC ANEMIA

Patients with SCD have chronic compensated hemolytic anemia because sickled RBCs undergo hemolysis after about 17 days. Their **baseline hemoglobin level is usually between 8-10 g/dL and** hematocrit level between 20-30%. Reticulocytosis is common with reticulocyte counts usually being in the 3-15% range. Peripheral blood smears can also show Howell-Jolly bodies. **Management for chronic compensated hemolytic anemia includes folic acid supplementation and regular CBC monitoring.**

APLASTIC CRISIS

This occurs when erythropoiesis transiently stops and causes an abrupt decrease in RBC precursors, which causes a **drop in the patient's reticulocyte count and hemoglobin level.** The most common cause of aplastic crisis is **parvovirus B19.** Management for aplastic crisis typically **requires blood transfusions.**

SPLENIC SEQUESTRATION CRISIS

Splenic sequestration crisis is when the patient's **RBCs are pooled into the spleen,** which presents as the patient having an enlarging spleen with a decrease in their baseline hemoglobin level that can lead to hypovolemic shock and death. **Patients commonly die before they can be transfused, but if they survive, then a splenectomy is usually done** to prevent a future recurrent episode.

VASO-OCCLUSIVE PAIN

Sickled RBCs have a higher chance of causing vaso-occlusion, which commonly presents as pain in patients with SCD. Common triggers for pain include cold temperatures, low humidity, wind, stress, menses, and dehydration. Pain can occur in chest, back, abdomen, or extremities. **The gold standard for pain assessment in SCD is the patient's report. The management for pain in patients with SCD is an individualized pain protocol** that allows most pain to be managed at home. If the pain cannot be managed at home with oral opioids, then the patient is instructed to go to the hospital for emergent care. **Hydroxyurea is a home medication that is used to prevent vaso-occlusive pain episodes.**

MULTIORGAN FAILURE

Multiorgan failure can occur in patients who present with an acute pain episode. For patients with SCD presenting with multiorgan failure, they should **immediately receive exchange transfusion therapy.**

NEUROLOGIC COMPLICATIONS

Patients with SCD have a higher risk of stroke, with ischemic strokes being more common in children than hemorrhagic stroke. **For stroke prevention**, a transcranial Doppler can be used for risk assessment and then a magnetic resonance angiography can be done for selective screening. Patients who are at risk for a stroke, or have had a stroke before, can be **managed with chronic prophylactic transfusions.** Patients with SCD are also at **higher risk of seizures**.

CARDIOPULMONARY COMPLICATIONS

ACUTE CHEST SYNDROME (ACS)

ACS is diagnosed when then patient has a **new pulmonary infiltrate in the setting of** any of the following symptoms:

- Fever
- Chest pain
- Cough
- Wheezing
- Respiratory distress
- Hypoxemia

Acute management for ACS includes analgesia, oxygen, transfusion, antibiotics, bronchodilators, and incentive spirometry. **For prevention to reduce the risk of ACS, consider** prophylactic antibiotics, vaccines, hydroxyurea, transfusions if hydroxyurea therapy fails, and hematopoietic cell transplantation if a donor is available. Although patients with SCD have a higher risk of asthma, having **asthma also increases the risk of ACS.**

PULMONARY HYPERTENSION

A high pulmonary artery pressure is diagnostic of pulmonary hypertension. Pulmonary hypertension symptoms are usually not specific such as chest pain, reduced exercise tolerance, chronic dyspnea, or presyncope. **A transthoracic Doppler echocardiogram should be done to obtain a baseline for all children who are at least 8 years old and then continue a routine screening for pulmonary hypertension every 1-3 years.**

RENAL COMPLICATIONS

Renal problems leading to renal insufficiency is common in patients with SCD. **For prevention of renal complications** avoid unnecessary nephrotoxic medications (e.g., NSAIDS), treat hypertension with medications that are not diuretics to avoid dehydration that can trigger a vaso-occlusive episode, and maintain a good hydration status during hospitalizations or when the patient has to use contrast for any imaging studies. **For screening, patients who are 3-5 years old should get baseline labs including** a chemistry (for baseline creatinine) and a urinalysis (for baseline urine protein and albumin).

SKELETAL COMPLICATIONS

DACTYLITIS

Dactylitis is vaso-occlusion of the hands and feet that causes pain and typically occurs in infants and children up to 4 years old. **Management of dactylitis includes** hydration, warm packs, analgesics, and considering hydroxyurea initiation.

OSTEOPOROSIS

Patients with SCD have a higher risk of vitamin D deficiency and osteoporosis because of increased erythropoietic activity. Patients **should be taking vitamin D and calcium** supplements. Patients with SCD should also **have vitamin D levels checked annually and get a bone density scan done every 1-3 years starting at 12 years of age.**

OSTEOMYELITIS

Patients with SCD have an increased risk of osteomyelitis, especially of the long bone in multiple areas. Although S. aureus is the most common cause of osteomyelitis in patients without SCD, **the most common cause of osteomyelitis in patients with SCD is Salmonella species.** Bone imaging and cultures can help differentiate osteomyelitis pain from vaso-occlusive pain.

OTHER COMPLICATIONS

RETINOPATHY

Occlusion and ischemia of the retinal artery can cause retinopathy in patients with SCD. **Children should begin having an ophthalmologic exam done annually starting at 10 years old.**

PRIAPISM

Priapism is an unwanted, prolonged, and painful erection due to vaso-occlusion in patients with SCD. **Parents should receive anticipatory guidance about priapism before the patient is 2 years old.** Priapism typically lasts for more than 30 minutes. **For "major" episodes of priapism lasting $\geq$ 4 hours, the patient should be taken to the emergency room** for immediate medical treatment due to the risk of ischemia that may cause permanent damage of the penis.

GROWTH AND DEVELOPMENT

Children with SCD commonly have delayed puberty (delayed menarche in females) and impaired growth. **As a result, their nutrition and environmental factors should be evaluated along with an endocrinology evaluation if their growth trajectory is decreased.**

PSYCHOSOCIAL ISSUES

Since SCD is a chronic disease that often presents with chronic pain, functional impairment and mental health issues such as anxiety and depression are common. As a result, **physicians should provide support by helping patients develop healthy coping strategies and providing resources for mental health help.**

REFERENCES

https://www.uptodate.com/contents/overview-of-the-clinical-manifestations-of-sickle-cell-disease
https://www.uptodate.com/contents/sickle-cell-disease-in-infancy-and-childhood-routine-health-care-maintenance-and-anticipatory-guidance

Topic 42: Staring Spells in Children – Planning the Evaluation
Plan the evaluation of a child with staring spells

BACKGROUND

Staring spells can either be due to pseudoabsence (nonepileptic) or absence (epileptic). Since absence seizures can be treated, it is important to differentiate pseudoabsence from absence staring spells.

PSEUDOABSENCE STARING SPELLS

Staring spells from pseudoabsence events can occur in children with ADHD, autism, intellectual disabilities, and sometimes in children who are otherwise normal. Boredom and being inactive can trigger nonepileptic staring spells in children (e.g., when they are sitting in class or watching videos). These episodes can usually be interrupted with either a vocal or tactile stimulus. It is very rare for nonepileptic staring episodes to occur during physical activity, and they never occur with motor signs, such as myoclonus or automatisms (lip-smacking, chewing, swallowing, etc.). **EEG will be normal at rest and may show generalized high-voltage slow activity with hyperventilation.**

CHILDHOOD ABSENCE SEIZURES

Childhood absence seizures typically begin around 4-10 years of age. Staring spells from absence seizures can be triggered in the safety of a primary care outpatient setting. **The patient is asked to hyperventilate for at least three minutes to provoke an episode**. The child will stop hyperventilating and stare, usually with the eyes slowly looking upward. The **trunk may begin to extend** and cause the patient to slowly lean backwards while sitting, therefore the physician should make sure the patient does not fall over. The facial muscles, head, or arms could have **myoclonic jerks with a low amplitude of three per second. Automatisms are usually common.** Patients have no recollection of anything that happened during the episode. The seizure typically lasts for only a few seconds but may last up to 20 seconds. **An EEG taken during the seizure will show a classic 3 Hz spike-and-wave pattern.**

Beware that hyperventilating can cause altered consciousness and decreased cerebral blood flow in some healthy children. **The EEG in a healthy child with nonepileptic staring spells after hyperventilating will be normal and will only show generalized high-voltage slow activity.**

OTHER LESS COMMON CAUSES OF STARING SPELLS

JUVENILLE ABSENCE EPILEPSY (JAE)
Patients with JAE can also present with absence seizures, but the age of onset (10-11 years of age) is later than that of childhood absence seizures. Some patients may also have **myoclonic seizures or generalized tonic clonic seizures**, which are not commonly seen with childhood absence seizures.

JUVENILLE MYOCLONIC EPILEPSY (JME)
Patients with JME **can initially present with absence seizures several years prior** to presenting with myoclonic seizures or generalized tonic clonic seizures. The EEG during their absence seizure phase will typically have a slightly **higher frequency such as 4-5 Hz instead of the 3 Hz** typically seen with childhood absence seizures.

GLUT1 DEFICIENCY SYNDROME
These patients can initially present with staring episodes prior to 4 years of age. CSF glucose levels can be low and **genetic testing** for SLC2A1 can confirm the diagnosis. Children may also have developmental delay and generalized epilepsy.

REFERENCES

https://www.uptodate.com/contents/nonepileptic-paroxysmal-disorders-in-children
https://www.uptodate.com/contents/childhood-absence-epilepsy

Topic 43: Status Epilepticus – Recognizing and Planning Initial Management
Recognize and plan initial management of status epilepticus

BACKGROUND
If status epilepticus continues for $\geq$ 30 minutes, the patient can suffer long-term neurologic consequences, such as neuronal injuries, neuronal network changes, or even neuronal death.

RECOGNIZING STATUS EPILEPTICUS
Status epilepticus is a clinical diagnosis and is **defined as either a single seizure that lasts longer than 5 minutes, or frequent seizures with no interictal return to the patient's clinical baseline at 5 minutes**. Such patients need **immediate assessment and treatment** in an acute care setting (e.g., the ER).

Patients in status epilepticus should undergo an urgent focused evaluation. **A focused history should seek to obtain the following information:**
- Any pre-hospital anti-seizure medications that were given
- Prior history of seizures
- Possible triggers for a seizure (fever, trauma, changes in medications, toxin exposures)
- Current medications
- History of anti-seizure medications used
- Which anti-seizure medications helped previously
- Other active medical issues or diagnoses (hypoglycemia or hyponatremia)
- Medical allergies

After assessing the patient's airway, breathing, circulation, and vital signs, a focused physical exam should be done looking for:
- Signs of head trauma (lacerations, swelling, etc.)
- Signs of sepsis or meningitis (fever, rash, poor perfusion, etc.)
- Characteristics of the seizure

INITIAL MANAGEMENT OF STATUS EPILEPTICUS

AIRWAY AND BREATHING
Patients should have their airway maintained either though positioning, jaw thrust, or placing a nasopharyngeal or oropharyngeal airway. A Yankauer should be used to **suction any secretions** with another large-bore suction device ready to be used in case the patient vomits. **100% oxygen** should be given with the patient's oxygen saturation levels being monitored by **pulse oximetry**. If the patient begins to have transient apnea or transient hypoxemia, the physician can use bag-mask ventilation.

The patient should receive **rapid sequence endotracheal intubation with mechanical ventilation if they start to have any of the following:**
- An airway that is no longer able to be maintained
- Inadequate ventilation
- Apnea
- Hypoxemia
- 30 minutes of seizure activity

CIRCULATION AND VASCULAR ACCESS

Since patients in status epilepticus **need labs and medications in a timely manner**, it is important to **establish peripheral IV access as quickly as possible**. If IV access is unable to be obtained within 5 minutes of the initial attempt, then anti-seizure medications should be given using an **alternative route such as rectal, intranasal, intramuscular, or intraosseous**. If the patient is hypotensive, a rapid IV infusion of isotonic normal saline or Ringer lactate should be given. The physician should keep in mind that a patient's heart rate and blood pressure may be temporarily elevated during status epilepticus, but this does not typically require treatment since there should be resolution once the seizure stops.

INITIAL LABS, STUDIES, AND IMAGING
LABS
Patients should have the following labs obtained:
- Plasma glucose **and** a rapid finger-stick glucose (treat hypoglycemia before using anti-seizure medications)
- Chemistries, including calcium levels (correct hyponatremia and other electrolyte disorders while also treating seizures)
- Anti-seizure medication levels (if patient is on any)
- Urine and blood toxicology screens if poisoning or substance use is suspected
- Qualitative pregnancy test in postmenarchal females

STUDIES

An urgent portable EEG should be done if there is uncertainty on whether the patient is truly seizing. **An EEG is not necessary for every patient**, but it can be helpful in evaluating any background activity in a patient who was in status epilepticus and recently stopped seizing.

IMAGING

Neuroimaging is usually not recommended immediately. It can be deferred until the patient has been stabilized to see if there is a possible structural cause for the seizure(s).

EMERGENCY TREATMENT

As mentioned above, address **hypoglycemia** prior to administering anti-seizure medications. Treat with seizure medications and address **electrolyte abnormalities** simultaneously since electrolyte replacements take time. Fevers can lower the threshold for seizures, so address febrile children with seizures with **prompt antipyretics**.

For patients who are at least 4 weeks old, anti-seizure medications are usually given as follows for a patient in status epilepticus:
- **Benzodiazepine** (lorazepam, diazepam, or midazolam) given immediately and repeat after 10 minutes if needed.
- **Long-acting, non-benzodiazepine medication** can be given if the second dose if benzodiazepine was ineffective (e.g., levetiracetam, phenytoin, fosphenytoin, or valproic acid)
- **Continuous infusion of midazolam or pentobarbital** is given in conjunction with another different anti-seizure medication if the patient is still seizing after 30 minutes, two benzodiazepine doses, and one non-benzodiazepine anti-seizure medication.

If a continuous infusion of anti-seizure medication is needed:
- Intubate the patient
- Transfer to the ICU
- Placed on continuous EEG monitoring
- Consult a neurologist

REFERENCES

https://www.uptodate.com/contents/management-of-convulsive-status-epilepticus-in-children

Topic 44: Thrombophilic Disorders – Recognizing the Complications and Implications

Recognize the complications and implications of thrombophilic disorders

BACKGROUND

Inherited thrombophilia (IT) is defined as when a patient is predisposed to developing a venous thromboembolism (VTE) due to genetic risk factors. **The most common genetic causes for thrombophilic disorders include:**

- Factor V Leiden mutation
- Protein C deficiency
- Protein S deficiency
- Antithrombin deficiency
- Prothrombin G20210A mutation

A venous thromboembolism can manifest as a deep vein thrombosis (DVT), pulmonary embolisms (PE), renal vein thrombosis (RVT), portal vein thrombosis (PVT), or cerebral venous thrombosis (CVT).

CLINICAL IMPLICATIONS

If a patient tests positive for an inherited thrombophilia, **special attention must be provided during the management of their care in these situations:**

- Selecting a method for contraception
- Pregnancy
- Surgeries
- Traumas
- Other situations that are considered high-risk for thrombosis

CONTRACEPTIVE COUNSELING

Estrogen containing contraceptives (e.g., the combined oral contraceptive pills, transdermal patch, or vaginal ring) significantly increase the risk of VTE from baseline. Progestin-only contraceptives, like the oral pill, injection, intrauterine device (IUD), and subdermal implant do not significantly increase the risk of VTE from baseline. Non-hormonal, reversible contraceptives like the copper IUD, condoms, and diaphragms do not increase the risk of VTE since they do not have any effect on hemostasis.

PREGNANCY

Since pregnancy increases the risk of VTE, adolescents should be counseled about the risks of VTE from both pregnancy and birth control so they can make an informed decision weighing the risks and benefits of each. **There are also fetal and neonatal risks in the context of Inherited thrombophilias including** fetal demise, cerebral palsy, preterm birth, perinatal stroke, and growth restriction.

COMPLICATIONS OF THROMBOPHILIC DISORDERS

DEEP VEIN THROMBOSIS (DVT)

LOWER EXTREMITY DVT

Children with a lower extremity DVT will usually complain of unilateral pain in either their leg, buttock, inguinal area, or abdomen. Other associated symptoms can include leg swelling or discoloration. Due to the swelling, the affected leg's calf can have a larger diameter than the unaffected leg.

UPPER EXTREMITY DVT

Children rarely get upper extremity DVT. If they do, it usually presents as **unilateral arm and hand swelling and discoloration**. Patients may complain of pain in either the arm, hand, neck, shoulder, or axilla of the affected side. If the superior vena cava is affected, then swelling of the face may occur.

PULMONARY EMBOLISM (PE)

Although a PE is rare in children, it can occur in severely sick children and should be included in the differential diagnosis if a child's cardiorespiratory status deteriorates. **Symptoms may include** tachypnea, tachycardia, hypoxia, pleuritic chest pain, acute dyspnea, cough, and sudden collapse. Patients with a PE may also display symptoms of a DVT.

RENAL VEIN THROMBOSIS (RVT)

SLE, nephrotic syndrome, and renal transplantation can increase the risk of RVT in children. **Patients with an RVT may have symptoms such as** anuria, hematuria, proteinuria, and vomiting.

PORTAL VEIN THROMBOSIS (PVT)

The risk of PVT in children with thrombophilic disorders increases with antiphospholipid syndrome, sickle cell disease, splenectomy, liver transplantation, chemotherapy, and infections. **Patients with a PVT may have symptoms including** an acute abdomen or the stigmata of chronic portal hypertension (e.g., splenomegaly or GI bleeding from esophageal varices).

CEREBRAL VENOUS THROMBOSIS (CVT)

Patients with thrombophilic disorders are at an **increased risk of CVT with** head trauma, lumbar puncture, or surgery. **Patients with a CVT may have symptoms including** headache (with or without emesis), papilledema, vision problems, focal deficits, seizures, or signs of diffuse brain injury or encephalopathy (e.g., changes in mental status, multifocal signs, coma).

REFERENCES
https://www.uptodate.com/contents/thrombophilia-testing-in-children-and-adolescents
https://www.uptodate.com/contents/contraception-counseling-for-women-with-inherited-thrombophilias
https://www.uptodate.com/contents/inherited-thrombophilias-in-pregnancy
https://www.uptodate.com/contents/venous-thrombosis-and-thromboembolism-vte-in-children-risk-factors-clinical-manifestations-and-diagnosis
https://www.uptodate.com/contents/cerebral-venous-thrombosis-etiology-clinical-features-and-diagnosis

Topic 45: Vaping or E-cigarette Use – Understanding the Health Risks
Understand the health risks of vaping or e-cigarette use

Exposure to nicotine and other aerosol components from vaping or e-cigarettes poses potential adverse health risks. Although the consequences of chronic vaping or e-cigarette use are not entirely known, they do contain toxic chemicals and carcinogenic compounds. Additionally, the devices themselves pose potential risks of harm.

NORMALIZING SMOKING BEHAVIOR

E-cigarettes were designed and promoted to appeal to youths and their use can normalize smoking behavior, which can lead to conventional cigarette use. **As the rate for e-cigarette usage has increased, so has the rate of regular cigarette use**.

NICOTINE EXPOSURE

Nicotine exposure results in e-cigarettes being considered a **gateway to nicotine dependence** that can later possibly **lead to tobacco use**. Pod-based devices use a high concentration of nicotine salts, which can be addicting. Nicotine is known to cause **increased heart rates, coronary vasoconstriction**, and an overall **increase in myocardial work**.

Nicotine withdrawal can present with symptoms such as irritability, anxiety, depression, tremors, insomnia, anger, or difficulty concentrating.

E-CIGARETTE COMPOSITION

The **liquid** in e-cigarette devices includes **nicotine, propylene glycol, glycerin, and flavoring chemicals like diacetyl and benzaldehyde**. The device heats this liquid into an **aerosol**, which then produces more **toxins and carcinogens**. **Acrolein** is one such toxin. **Acetaldehyde, formaldehyde, and propylene oxide** are the substances that created which are known to be, or likely to be, **carcinogenic**. Furthermore, the **metal coils** in the device can also release **small metallic particles like lead** into the aerosol.

AEROSOL/VAPOR EXPOSURE

Exposure to aerosols and vapors of e-cigarettes can increase the risk of **respiratory issues such as** acute eosinophilic pneumonia, hypersensitivity pneumonitis, asthma, or chronic bronchitis that presents with symptoms such as chronic cough and phlegm production.

Flavoring chemicals such as diacetyl and benzaldehyde are associated with **respiratory irritation**. E-cigarettes can also increase the risk of severe lung related injuries such **as E-cigarette or Vaping Associated Lung Injury (EVALI)**, which can eventually lead to respiratory failure. Symptoms of EVALI can include shortness of breath, cough, chest pain, pleuritic chest pain, hemoptysis, fever, chills, nausea, vomiting, diarrhea, and abdominal pain

INCREASED RISK OF COVID

Patients who use both e-cigarettes and regular cigarettes have an increased risk of COVID infection.

DEVICE RISKS

Device malfunction can cause **burns, explosive injuries, or chemical injuries** while the device is stored (such as in a pocket) or while it is being used. Exposure to the e-cigarette **liquid via oral/parenteral ingestion or skin contact can also be harmful and may cause** symptoms such as nausea, vomiting, tachycardia, seizures, lactic acidosis, lethargy, anoxic brain injury, or even death.

REFERENCES

https://www.uptodate.com/contents/vaping-and-e-cigarettes
https://www.uptodate.com/contents/e-cigarette-or-vaping-product-use-associated-lung-injury-evali
https://publications.aap.org/pediatricsinreview/article-abstract/41/3/152/35381

Featured Reading #1: Anxiety Disorders in Children and Adolescents - Assessment and Treatment

Walter HJ, Bukstein OG, Abright AR, Keable H, Ramtekkar U, Ripperger-Suhler J, Rockhill C. Clinical Practice Guideline for the Assessment and Treatment of Children and Adolescents With Anxiety Disorders. J Am Acad Child Adolesc Psychiatry. 2020 Oct;59(10)
https://pubmed.ncbi.nlm.nih.gov/32439401/

BACKGROUND

Anxiety is one of the most common psychiatric disorders in pediatrics and can range from a specific phobia, social anxiety, separation anxiety, agoraphobia, panic and generalized anxiety disorder. Although evidence-based treatment is available, less than half of youths who need mental health treatment receive it. Therefore, it is imperative for general pediatricians to be able to better identify, assess, and treat mental illness in youths.

ASSESSMENT OF ANXIETY

IDENTIFICATION

There is currently no empirically based recommendation for universal screening for anxiety in youths. For schools, and other child-serving settings, other freely available generalized social-emotional screening tools are available to standardize identification of concerns for anxiety,

The American Psychiatric Association (APA) created the **free parent and self-rated Level 1 Cross-Cutting Symptom Measures to screen** for many psychiatric disorders including anxiety.

EVALUATION

The DSM-5 has diagnostic criteria for 11 anxiety disorders. The most common are:

- **Separation Anxiety**: developmentally inappropriate, excessive worry, or distress associated with separation from a primary caregiver or major attachment figure
- **Selective Mutism**: absence of speech in certain social situations despite the presence of speech in other situations
- **Specific Phobia**: excessive fear or worry about a specific object or social situation
- **Social anxiety**: excessive fear or worry about being negatively evaluated by others in social situations
- **Panic**: abrupt surge of intense fear or discomfort characterized by recurrent unexpected panic attacks with physical and cognitive manifestations
- **Agoraphobia**: excessive fear or worry about being in situations in which the individual may be unable to escape or get help should panic-like or other overwhelming or embarrassing symptoms occur
- **Generalized Anxiety**: excessive, uncontrollable worries regarding numerous everyday situations or activities
- **Substance/Medication-Induced and Anxiety Due to Another Medical Condition**: anxiety in the context of substance/medication use or a physical illness
- **Other-specified and Unspecified**: Anxiety that does not fully meet criteria for a given anxiety disorder

DIFFERENTIAL DIAGNOSIS

- **Physical Medical Conditions:** hyperthyroidism, caffeinism, migraine, asthma, diabetes, chronic pain/illness, lead intoxication, hypoglycemic episodes, hypoxia, pheochromocytoma, central nervous system disorders, cardiac arrhythmias, cardiac valvular disease, systemic lupus erythematosus, allergic reactions, and dysmenorrhea. Labs are not routinely done when evaluating for anxiety, but glucose and thyroid levels can be checked if the patient has suggestive symptoms.
- **Mental Medical Conditions:** ADHD, depression, bipolar disorder, OCD, psychotic disorders, autism spectrum disorder, and learning disorders
- **Medications:** bronchodilators, nasal decongestants (sympathomimetics), antihistamines, steroids, dietary supplements, stimulants, antidepressants, antipsychotics, and benzodiazepine withdrawal.
- **Substance Use:** marijuana, cocaine, anabolic steroids, hallucinogens, phencyclidine, and withdrawal from nicotine, alcohol, and caffeine

INTERVIEW GUIDES, SYMPTOM SCALES, AND EXAM

- **Anxiety Disorders Interview Schedule (ADIS):** This is considered to be a gold standard in research settings for assessing childhood anxiety and addresses all DSM-IV anxiety disorders.
- **Symptom Scales:** These can be used to quantify pretreatment symptom severity to trend treatment response.
- **Exam:** Patients with anxiety can present with disheveled appearance, poor eye contact, poor engagement, clinginess, tremors, restlessness, hypervigilance, pressured speech, ruminating thoughts, worried thoughts, distractibility, irritability, agitation, and poor insight.
- **Anxiety Contributors:** These can include stressors, cultural upbringing, spirituality, gender/sexual orientation, development, education, family, and other social factors.

TREATMENT OF ANXIETY

SAFETY AND TREATMENT PLANNING

Patient safety should be assessed by evaluating for suicidal thoughts and behaviors, self-harm, risky behaviors, impulsivity, abuse, and neglect. Ensure that the patient is **not currently at risk, has caregiver supervision**, and is **able to follow up.** Informed consent for treatment should include the diagnosis, purpose of proposed treatment, risks and benefits of proposed treatment, risks and benefits of alternative treatments, and risks and benefits of declining treatment. Being respectful of cultural/spiritual values, beliefs, and attitudes toward treatment can enhance treatment effectiveness. The American Academy of Child and Adolescent Psychiatry (AACAP) recommends the following types of treatments for patients 6-18 years old with **social anxiety, generalized anxiety, separation anxiety, or panic disorder**:

- Cognitive Behavioral Therapy (CBT)
- Selective Serotonin Reuptake Inhibitors (SSRIs)
- Combination Treatment (CBT and an SSRI): This is preferentially over CBT or SSRI treatment alone
- Serotonin Norepinephrine Reuptake Inhibitors (SNRIs).

For patients with **specific phobias**, CBT is recommended.

REFERENCES

https://pubmed.ncbi.nlm.nih.gov/32439401/

Featured Reading #2: Asthma Management NIH Guidelines – 2020 Focused Updates

Cloutier MM, Teach SJ, Lemanske RF Jr, Blake KV. The 2020 Focused Updates to the NIH Asthma Management Guidelines: Key Points for Pediatricians. Pediatrics. 2021 Jun;147(6):e2021050286. doi: 10.1542/peds.2021-050286. Epub 2021 May 3. PMID: 33941586; PMCID: PMC8168603.
https://pubmed.ncbi.nlm.nih.gov/33941586

BACKGROUND

The 2020 Updates to the NIH Asthma Management Guidelines are the first updates since 2007. The updates had **three treatment options that were focused on**, including:

1. The use of intermittent inhaled corticosteroids (ICS) dosing with as-needed short-acting β2-agonist (SABA) for quick-relief therapy.
2. Single maintenance and reliever therapy (SMART).
3. Add-on long-acting muscarinic antagonist (LAMA) therapy.

Physicians should always assess for treatment adherence, correct inhaler technique, environmental triggers, and any comorbid conditions **before making any changes to step up a patient's care**.

INTERMITTENT INHALED CORTICOSTEROID (ICS)

CHILDREN 0 - 4 YEARS OLD WITH INTERMITTENT ASTHMA

- Recommend a **short course** of about 7 – 10 days of **daily ICS** with short acting beta-2 agonist **(SABA) as-needed when a viral respiratory tract infection starts** for children who had 3 or more episodes in their lifetime of viral-induced wheezing or 2 or more episodes in the past year who are asymptomatic between episodes.

CHILDREN 4 YEARS OLD OR OLDER WITH MILD TO MODERATE PERSISTENT ASTHMA

- **If adherent** with daily ICS by itself, **increasing the ICS dose short-term is not recommended**.
- **If not adherent** with ICS by itself, can **consider increasing the ICS dose short-term**.

CHILDREN 12 YEARS OLD OR OLDER WITH MILD PERSISTENT ASTHMA

- Consider shared decision making with families to have the patient use **as-needed ICS with SABA instead of daily ICS with as-needed SABA**.
- Since the importance of using daily ICS was previously emphasized, it may be difficult to reeducate families about switching from daily ICS to as-needed ICS.

SINGLE MAINTENANCE AND RELIEVER THERAPY (SMART)

SMART is both a daily and rescue therapy treatment that uses **ICS with Formoterol, which is a specific long-acting beta-2 agonist (LABA)**. Both medications are combined in a singular device. **SMART therapy is more effective** than daily ICS. It also **reduces rates of exacerbation, overall use of corticosteroids, and effects on growth rates**. SMART therapy is recommended for children 4 years old or older who are not well controlled on daily low or medium ICS use by itself.

ADD-ON LONG-ACTING MUSCARINIC ANTAGONIST (LAMA) THERAPY

CHILDREN 12 YEARS OLD OR OLDER

- For **moderate persistent asthma**, if SMART therapy (1st line treatment) or daily ICS-LABA (2nd line treatment) are not effective, then the **3rd line treatment is daily ICS-LAMA**.

- For **severe persistent asthma**, if ICS-LABA is not effective, then the **next step** would be to use a combination of three devices using **daily medium or high dose ICS-LABA plus LAMA with as-needed SABA**. Tiotropium is an example of a LAMA medication.

INDOOR ALLERGEN MITIGATION

Nonspecific indoor allergen mitigation is not recommended for routine asthma care. Allergen mitigation should only be used for patients exposed to a specific allergen that they are already sensitized to or became symptomatic after exposure. If used, then the intervention strategies should be individualized to the patient and comprise of multiple interventions, unless it is pest management, which can be recommended alone or as part of the multi-intervention strategy.

SUBCUTANEOUS IMMUNOTHERAPY (SCIT) AND SUBLINGUAL IMMUNOTHERAPY (SLIT)

SCIT and SLIT reduce the IgE-mediated response that asthma is associated with.

SCIT can be used in addition to the recommended standard treatment in children who are ≥ 5 years old with mild to moderate allergic asthma and wanting to decrease long-term use of medications. SCIT should not be given to those with severe asthma or uncontrolled persistent asthma. SCIT should only be given in a clinically monitored setting in case of any **adverse reactions**.

SLIT is not recommended for asthma treatment, but it may help those who have comorbid conditions such as allergic rhinitis.

FRACTIONAL EXHALED NITRIC OXIDE (FENO) TESTING

The nitric oxide (NO) found in an exhaled breath can **indirectly measure type 2 (eosinophilic) airway inflammation** in a safe and noninvasive way and provide supportive information to help diagnose and manage asthma. However, it requires the purchase of specialized equipment, and the results can be difficult to interpret. It should not be used in children ≤ 4 years of age.

It is not recommended to use FeNO testing alone to diagnose or manage asthma, but it **can help support the diagnosis of asthma** in children ≥ 5 years old if the diagnosis is uncertain.

FeNO testing can be used every 2-3 months to **supplement the monitoring of the asthma management plan** for children with an established asthma diagnosis, but it is not recommended to be used to assess compliance with treatment.

REFERENCES
https://www.ncbi.nlm.nih.gov/pmc/articles/PMC8168603

Featured Reading #3: Sudden Death in the Young

CC, Salerno JC, Berger S, Campbell R, Cannon B, Christiansen J, Moffatt K, Pflaumer A, Snyder CS, Srinivasan C, Valdes SO, Vetter VL, Zimmerman F; SECTION ON CARDIOLOGY AND CARDIAC SURGERY, PEDIATRIC AND CONGENITAL ELECTROPHYSIOLOGY SOCIETY (PACES) TASK FORCE ON PREVENTION OF SUDDEN DEATH IN THE YOUNG. Sudden Death in the Young: Information for the Primary Care Provider. Pediatrics. 2021 Jul;148(1):e2021052044. doi: 10.1542/peds.2021-052044. Epub 2021 Jun 21. PMID: 34155130.
https://pubmed.ncbi.nlm.nih.gov/34155130

BACKROUND

An update to the 2012 AAP policy statement addressing the prevention of sudden cardiac arrest or sudden cardiac death. Sudden cardiac arrest (SCA) is defined as a sudden, abrupt loss of heart function, breathing, and consciousness typically due to sustained ventricular tachycardia (VT) or ventricular fibrillation (VF). **Sudden cardiac death (SCD)** is defined as an unexpected natural death from a cardiac cause within a short time period.

Key takeaways from this update include:
- Pediatricians should be aware of the clinical history, family history, and physical exam findings that may increase the risk of SCA and SCD.
- An EKG read by a trained professional should be the first test in any patient suspected to be at risk for sudden cardiac arrest, and computer readings should not be accepted blindly.
- Screening for SCA should be done every 3 years for all children, **not just athletes**.
- No single screening method can capture all children at risk for SCA, but a 4-question screen (shared below) can help catch many, and it can be easily incorporated in pediatricians routine visits.
- Access to the following are critical in helping to reduce SCA: emergency action plans, CPR training in the community, AEDs
- Survivors of SCA, SCD, and their family members should undergo a thorough evaluation looking for a genetic etiology. This may need to be done at a specialized center for SCA.

DIFFERENTIAL DIAGNOSIS AND EVALUATION

Various diagnoses are discussed below. Regarding the evaluation, an **EKG should be the first test ordered when there is concern for potential sudden cardiac arrest**. It should be **read by a trained professional** (accepting the computer interpretation blindly is not acceptable).

CARDIOMYOPATHIES

Cardiomyopathies may include dilated cardiomyopathy, hypertrophic cardiomyopathy, restrictive cardiomyopathy, or arrhythmogenic cardiomyopathy. These **can result in** life-threatening arrhythmias including ventricular tachycardia (VT). Obtain an **echocardiogram and/or MRI** for diagnosis.

CHANNELOPATHIES

Look for different types of channelopathies including long QT syndrome, short QT syndrome, Brugada syndrome, catecholaminergic polymorphic ventricular tachycardia, or idiopathic ventricular fibrillation. If suspecting long QT syndrome or Brugada syndrome, obtain a **detailed medication history** (especially, antibiotics, antifungals, or stimulants for ADHD) and check the following sites (https://crediblemeds.org or https://brugadadrugs.org) for any medication contraindications to channelopathies. **Obtain an EKG for diagnosis**.

CONGENITAL HEART DISEASE

Congenital heart disease results in a **high risk for arrhythmias** including ventricular tachycardia (VT). Obtain an **echocardiogram** for diagnosis of the congenital heard disease and an **EKG** to evaluate arrhythmias.

WOLFF-PARKINSON-WHITE SYNDROME

This results in **supraventricular tachycardia (SVT), or rarely, atrial fibrillation (AF) leading to ventricular fibrillation (VF)**. Obtain an EKG for diagnosis and consult with a **pediatric electrophysiologist and consider a curative ablation** procedure for treatment.

COMMOTIO CORDIS

This results in **ventricular fibrillation (VF) due to a sudden impact to the chest**. This is the most **common in baseball** when a ball hits an athlete's chest. Obtain an **echocardiogram and EKG** and the child can return to sports if no cardiac disease is identified.

ANOMALOUS CORONARY ARTERIES

Have a high suspicion of this in patients with **syncope or atypical chest pain**. Obtain an **echocardiogram, CT, MRI, or coronary angiography** for diagnosis. Treatment is surgical unroofing or reimplantation of the anomalous coronary.

AORTOPATHIES

These include Marfan syndrome, familial thoracic aortic aneurysm and dissection, bicuspid aortic valve with aortic dilation, Loeys-Dietz syndrome, and Ehler-Danlos syndrome. Aortopathies **can lead to an increased risk of aortic dilation and dissection**. Avoid isometric exercise (Valsalva maneuver) and collision sports.

PRIMARY PREVENTION

All patients (even non-athletes) should be screened at routine visits at a minimum of every 3 years. Any positive response to the following preparticipation evaluation (PPE) screens require further cardiovascular evaluation prior to sports clearance.

- The **American Heart Association (AHA)** recommends an **annual 14-point history and physical screening for athletic participation** known as the preparticipation evaluation (PPE).
- The **American Academy of Pediatrics (AAP)** recommends a **modified, 4 question (PPE) addressed every 2-3 years for all patients aged 6-to-21 years old** (even non-athletes). The 4 questions include:

  - During exercise or in response to sudden loud noises, have you passed out, fainted, or had an unexplained seizure suddenly without warning?
  - Have you had exercise related shortness of breath or chest pain?
  - Any unexpected sudden deaths before age 50 years old in your immediate or more distant relatives?
  - Any relation to someone with hypertrophic cardiomyopathy or hypertrophic obstructive cardiomyopathy, Marfan syndrome, arrhythmogenic cardiomyopathy, Long QT syndrome, Short QT syndrome, Brugada syndrome, catecholaminergic polymorphic

ventricular tachycardia, or anyone younger than 50 with a pacemaker or implantable defibrillator?

SECONDARY PREVENTION

Prompt recognition of cardiac arrest with high-quality CPR and early defibrillation with AEDs saves lives. Survival rates decrease by 10% with every minute delay in CPR and AED administration. Schools are a great place to develop a **cardiac emergency response plan (CERP)** which include:

- Collapse-to-EMS call time of < 1 minute.
- Collapse-to-first shock time of < 3 minutes if AED is on-site.
- Practice emergency response drills at least 2 times per year with at least 10% of regular staff and 50% of physical education staff trained with current CPR and AED certification.

RETURN TO ACTIVITY AFTER CARDIAC ARREST

REVERSIBLE CAUSES

Reversible causes of cardiac arrest include hypoxia, hypokalemia, hyperkalemia, hypothermia, hyperthermia, hypovolemia, tension pneumothorax, tamponade, thrombosis, and toxins (remember the H's and T's!). There should be **no athletic participation after these causes until cleared at a 3-month reevaluation** by a pediatric cardiologist or electrophysiologist.

NON-REVERSIBLE CAUSES (ARRTHYMIAS FROM VT OR VF)

Arrhythmias including ventricular tachycardia and ventricular fibrillation are non-reversible causes of cardiac arrest. Strongly consider implantable cardioverter-defibrillator (ICD) placement. Allow patients to return to low-level dynamic and static activities, such as golf and bowling, after **3-months** of not requiring ICD intervention to treat episodes of VT or VF. Return to higher-intensity activities at that time may also be considered after discussion with the family about the increased risk of ICD shocks and also the risk of potential device trauma with certain types of activities.

DEATH AFTER CARDIAC ARREST

Sudden cardiac death (SCD) occurs in about 2,000 patients < 25 years old in the US every year. After sudden cardiac death, have a skilled medical examiner examine the cardiac anatomy by **autopsy and consider molecular genetic testing** if no structural causes are found on autopsy. A **structural cardiac cause is present on autopsy in most cases** of SCD. Unexplained SCD is often attributed to cardiac arrhythmia. Prepare the family by utilizing the *HeartRescue Project's Life After SCA Initiative* (http://www.heartrescueproject.com/survivor-support/). **Evaluate remaining family members** as up to 30% of first-degree relatives have evidence of inherited cardiac disease. **Test first-degree relatives with an EKG**, exercise stress test if old enough, echocardiogram +/- genetic testing and referral to a pediatric cardiologist or electrophysiologist.

REFERENCE
https://pubmed.ncbi.nlm.nih.gov/34155130/

Featured Reading #4: Well-Appearing Febrile Infants 8 to 60 Days Old - Evaluation and Management

Pantell RH, Roberts KB, Adams WG, Dreyer BP, Kuppermann N, O'Leary ST, Okechukwu K, Woods CR Jr; SUBCOMMITTEE ON FEBRILE INFANTS. Evaluation and Management of Well-Appearing Febrile Infants 8 to 60 Days Old. Pediatrics. 2021 Aug;148(2):e2021052228. doi: 10.1542/peds.2021-052228. Epub 2021 Jul 19. Erratum in: Pediatrics. 2021 Nov;148(5): PMID: 34281996.
https://pubmed.ncbi.nlm.nih.gov/34281996

BACKGROUND

In 2021, the AAP published a guideline for evaluating and managing term infants ages 8-60 days old who are presenting with a fever of at least 38°C, but are otherwise well-appearing. The preferences and values of the parents should be part of the shared decision-making process when appropriate. **The three algorithms for this guideline are stratified by 3 age groups.**

8-21 DAYS OLD WITH FEVER

If the patient has a fever of at least 38°C and is otherwise well-appearing with no obvious source of infection, then the physician should obtain a urinalysis, blood culture, and do a lumbar puncture (LP). Inflammatory markers (IM) may be obtained.

If the patient has an increased risk of HSV, the physician should send HSV studies and then start IV antibiotics and acyclovir. The patient should be observed in the hospital. **If a pathogen or source is identified**, then the infection should be treated. **If a pathogen or source is not identified**, then the antibiotics and acyclovir should be discontinued if the culture results are all negative at 24-36 hours and the HSV PCR results are negative. The patient can then be discharged from the hospital and continue to be managed for the duration of their illness.

If the patient does not have an increased risk of HSV, the physician should start IV antibiotics without acyclovir. The patient should be observed in the hospital. **If a pathogen or source is identified**, then the infection should be treated. **If a pathogen or source is not identified**, then the antibiotics should be discontinued if the culture results are all negative at 24-36 hours. **If HSV PCR testing was done**, wait until the results are available and negative to discharge the patient.

22-28 DAYS OLD WITH FEVER

If the patient has a fever of at least 38°C and is otherwise well-appearing with no obvious source of infection, then the physician should obtain a urinalysis, blood culture, and inflammatory markers.

If the urinalysis results are positive, the physician should send a urine culture from either a bladder catheterization or a suprapubic aspiration (SPA) sample.

Once the urine culture is sent, or if the urinalysis results are negative, the physician should then interpret the inflammatory markers.

- **If the inflammatory markers are abnormal**, the physician should do an LP. **If CSF was obtained**, the results should be interpreted.
  - o **If CSF was normal**, the physician can decide to have the patient be observed either at home or the hospital. **If the patient will be observed at home**, they should be given parenteral antibiotics and be reassessed in 24 hours. **If the patient will be observed in the hospital**, the physician can consider giving parenteral antibiotics.
  - o **If CSF was unable to be obtained, or the CSF showed pleocytosis, or is not able to be interpreted**, parenteral antibiotics should be given and the patient should be observed in the hospital.
- **If the inflammatory markers are normal**, the physician can consider doing an LP.
  - o **If an LP is done**, the above steps of doing an LP if the inflammatory markers were abnormal should also be done.
  - o **If an LP is not done**, the patient should be observed in the hospital and the physician can consider giving parenteral antibiotics.

If a pathogen or source is identified, then the infection should be treated. **If a pathogen or source is not identified**, then the antibiotics should be discontinued if the culture results are all negative at 24-36 hours. **If the HSV PCR results were sent**, they should wait until those results are also negative. The patient can then be discharged from the hospital and continue to be managed for the duration of their illness.

29-60 DAYS OLD WITH FEVER
If the patient has a fever of at least 38°C, but is otherwise well-appearing with no evident source of infection, then the physician should obtain a urinalysis, blood culture, and inflammatory markers.

If the inflammatory markers are elevated, then the physician should send a urine culture from either a bladder catheterization or suprapubic aspiration if the urinalysis is positive. The physician can also consider doing an LP.

- **If an LP is not done, or the CSF results are unable to be interpreted**, the physician should give parenteral antibiotics and consider observing either at home or in the hospital.
- **If CSF results are positive**, the patient should be given parenteral antibiotics and observed in the hospital.
- **If CSF results are negative (regardless of the urinalysis results)**, then the physician can **consider** giving either parenteral or oral antibiotics and consider observing either at home or in the hospital since the inflammatory markers are elevated.

If the inflammatory markers are not elevated, then the physician should look at the urinalysis results.

- **If the urinalysis is positive**, the physician should send a urine culture from either a bladder catheterization or suprapubic aspiration. **An LP does not need to done. The patient should be given an oral antibiotic**, be observed at home, and follow up in 12-24 hours.
- **If the urinalysis is negative**, the physician does not need to do an LP. The patient does not need any antibiotics. The patient is to be observed at home and follow up in 24-36 hours.

If the pathogen or source is identified at 24-36 hours and is limited only to the urine, then the patient should complete treatment with oral antibiotics, be discharged from the hospital, and continue to be managed for the duration of their illness.

If the pathogen or source is not limited to the urine, then the pathogen or source should be treated.

If the pathogen or source is not identified at 24-36 hours, then the patient should discontinue their antibiotics, be discharged from the hospital, and continue to be managed for the duration of their illness.

REFERENCE
https://pubmed.ncbi.nlm.nih.gov/34281996

CME OPPORTUNITIES

DID YOU KNOW THAT YOU MAY QUALIFY FOR A $2000 CASH REBATE?

PLUS...

200 CME CREDITS
200 MOC PART 2 POINTS

VISIT THE FOLLOWING LINK & LEARN MORE NOW!
www.pbrlinks.com/MOCA-CME